Let's Read Aloud & Learn English:

Going Abroad

音読で学ぶ基礎英語≪海外生活編≫

By
Teruhiko Kadoyama
Simon Capper
Toshiaki Endo

 SEIBIDO

photographs by
iStockphoto

音声ファイルのダウンロード／ストリーミング

CD マーク表示がある箇所は、音声を弊社 HP より無料でダウンロード／ストリーミングすることができます。下記 URL の書籍詳細ページに音声ダウンロードアイコンがございますのでそちらから自習用音声としてご活用ください。

http://seibido.co.jp/ad599

Let's Read Aloud & Learn English: Going Abroad

Copyright © 2021 by Teruhiko Kadoyama, Simon Capper, Toshiaki Endo

リンガポルタのご案内　　　LINGUAPORTA

リンガポルタ連動テキストをご購入の学生さんは、「リンガポルタ」を無料でご利用いただけます！

本テキストで学習していただく内容に準拠した問題を、オンライン学習システム「リンガポルタ」で学習していただくことができます。PCだけでなく、スマートフォンやタブレットでも学習できます。単語や文法、リスニング力などをよりしっかり身に付けていただくため、ぜひ積極的に活用してください。
リンガポルタの利用にはアカウントとアクセスコードの登録が必要です。登録方法については下記ページにアクセスしてください。

https://www.seibido.co.jp/linguaporta/register.html

本テキスト「Let's Read Aloud & Learn English: Going Abroad」のアクセスコードは下記です。

7226-2045-1231-0365-0003-006c-1GNQ-PR5R

・リンガポルタの学習機能（画像はサンプルです。また、すべてのテキストに以下の4つの機能が用意されているわけではありません）

多肢選択

空所補充（音声を使っての聞き取り問題も可能）

単語並びかえ（マウスや手で単語を移動）

マッチング（マウスや手で単語を移動）

は し が き

　本書は、「音読」や「筆写」といった、一見地味ですが確実に英語力アップにつながる練習法を取り入れた総合英語テキストで、『音読で始める基礎英語』シリーズの第 4 弾に当たるものです。前 3 作同様、基礎的な語彙や文法の確認に重点を置いていますが、本作は大学生の主人公がアメリカにホームステイに出かけるというストーリー仕立てになっていますので、海外旅行や語学研修に関連した表現を数多く学ぶことができるはずです。

　「英語をペラペラ話せるようになりたい」と願う人は多いですが、授業や自宅での学習で実際にどれだけ英語を音読する練習をしてきたでしょうか？　何度も音読しなければやはり英語が口からすぐに出てくるようにはなりませんし、実際に英文を書いてみるという作業は表現を確認し定着させる上で非常に効果的です。デジタル全盛な時代にあえてこうしたアナログ的な練習方法を提唱するのは、やはり 1 番効果が実感しやすい方法だと思うからです。

　しかし、本書はアナログ的な面だけを重視したテキストでは決してありません。本書は Web 英語学習システムの LINGUAPORTA（リンガポルタ）に対応していますので、パソコンやスマートフォンを使ったモバイル・ラーニングが可能です。アナログとデジタルのそれぞれ良い点を皆さんの英語学習に活かしてほしいと願っています。

　本書は 15 ユニットからなり、各ユニットの構成は次のようになっています。

- ■ **WARM-UP**：授業で聞く対話の中に出てくる重要単語や表現、そして文法項目を取り上げていますので、授業の予習としてやっておきましょう。
- ■ **LET'S LISTEN!**：ホームステイを舞台にした対話を聞いてみましょう。対話の大意が理解できているかを試す問題が用意されています。
- ■ **LET'S CHECK & READ ALOUD!**：空欄補充問題を設けていますので、LET'S LISTEN! で聞いた対話をもう 1 度聞いて空欄を埋めてみましょう。内容を確認したら、音読、そしてパートナーとロールプレイ（役割練習）をしてみましょう。QR コードからアクセスできるオンライン動画を用意していますので、ぜひ自宅学習でも積極的に取り入れてください。そうすればその効果が実感できることでしょう。
- ■ **GRAMMAR**：WARM-UP で取り上げた文法項目の確認問題です。文法に苦手意識のある方はこのページでしっかり復習をしておきましょう。
- ■ **LET'S READ!**：異文化理解に関するパッセージを読んでみましょう。大意が理解できているかを試す問題が用意されています。
- ■ **CHALLENGE YOURSELF!**：英語の資格試験としてよく知られている TOEIC Bridge® と似た形式のリスニング問題を用意しました。試験を意識した実践的な演習をしてみましょう。
- ■ **LET'S READ ALOUD & WRITE!**：最後に授業のまとめとして、学習した対話を音読筆写してみましょう。日本語訳だけを見ながら英文がスラスラと書けるようになることが目標です。
- ■ **LET'S REVIEW**：巻末に文法と表現の復習コーナーを用意しています。日本語の文を見てすぐさま対応する英文を言ってみるという Quick Response（即時反応）のトレーニングで、学習した内容がしっかり身についているかどうか確かめましょう。

　本書の刊行にあたっては、成美堂の佐野英一郎氏、そして編集部の工藤隆志氏、萩原美奈子氏に多大なご尽力を賜りました。衷心よりお礼申し上げます。

角山照彦
Simon Capper
遠藤利昌

Table of Contents

〈主な登場人物〉

Takashi

心理学を専攻する大学１年生

Beth

タカシの英語の先生

UNIT	タイトル	テーマ	文法	言語機能
09 p.56	I think I'm lost.	道案内	形容詞・副詞	援助を求める 道順を示す
10 p.62	Do you want me to take your picture?	観光地	不定詞	援助を申し出る 確認を求める
11 p.68	I've lost my phone.	遺失物取扱所	分詞	問題を述べる 確信を示す
12 p.74	I love roller coasters!	アミューズメント パーク	比較	賛同する 感想を述べる
13 p.80	Let me introduce my friend.	ホームパーティ	関係詞	人を紹介する 手みやげを渡す
14 p.86	I'd like to pay by credit card.	ショッピング	接続詞・前置詞	好みを述べる 意向を尋ねる
15 p.92	I'm looking forward to seeing you again.	空港での見送り	動名詞	意思を示す 話題を変える

 Let's Review ·················· p.98

* **巻末資料**（品詞の分類、文の要素と基本文型、人称代名詞の種類と格変化表、不規則動詞変化表、音節、発音記号の読み方、QR コードの URL 一覧）… p.113

Yoona

韓国からの留学生

Donna

タカシのホストマザー

UNIT 01 This is my first trip abroad.

文法 **be** 動詞

語学研修のためロサンゼルスに到着したタカシ
は、空港で入国審査を受けます。会話では、予定
を尋ねる表現や別れ際の挨拶を学びます。また、
文法では **be** 動詞（現在形・過去形）と疑問詞に
焦点を当てて学習します。

 Warm-up　　　　　　　　　　　　授業前に確認しておこう！

》***Vocabulary Preview***

1 ～ 10 の語句の意味として適切なものを a ～ j の中から選びましょう。　　🎵 1-02

1. landing card _____	a. 観光
2. alone _____	b. 旅行する
3. actually _____	c. 目的
4. stay _____	d. 入国管理（所）
5. flight _____	e. 海外に（へ）
6. sightseeing _____	f. 入国カード
7. abroad _____	g. 滞在する、滞在
8. travel _____	h. 実は、実際
9. immigration _____	i. 飛行便、空の旅
10. purpose _____	j. 1 人で

ビートに乗って 1 ～ 10 の語句を発音してみましょう。

》***Grammar Point : be*** 動詞

This <u>is</u> my first visit to the United States.　　（アメリカを訪れるのはこれが初めてです）
It <u>was</u> nice talking to you.　　　　　　　　　（お話しできてよかったです）

　be 動詞は名詞や形容詞、場所を表す語句が後に続いて「～である、～にいる」と
いう意味を表し、主語によっていろいろと形が変わります。また、「～だった、～に
いた」と過去を表す場合も同じく変化します。下の表の空欄に枠の中から適切な動詞
の形を選んで表を完成させましょう。

am ✓
is
are
was
were

話し手のことを
1 人称、
相手方を 2 人称、
それ以外の人たちを
3 人称と言います。

	主　　　　　　　　語		現在形	過去形
1 人称	単数（私）	I	*am*	
	複数（私たち）	we		
2 人称	単数（あなた）	you		
	複数（あなたたち）			
3 人称	単数（彼、彼女、それ）	he, she, it		
	複数（彼ら、それら）	they		

「～ではない」という否定文にするときは、be 動詞のすぐ後に not をつけます。また、「～ですか？」という疑問文にするには be 動詞を主語の前に持ってきます。下の例文の日本語訳を完成させながら確認しましょう。

A flight attendant's job is popular, but it <u>isn't</u> easy.

(_____)

<u>Is</u> this the check-in counter for flights to Los Angeles?

(_____)

is not = isn't,
are not = aren't
のように会話では短縮形がよく使われます。
ただし、I am not は通常 I'm not となります。
× I amn't

なお、疑問文を作る際には、when や where などの**疑問詞**がよく使われますが、これらは通常疑問文の始めに置かれます。下の表で確認した後、例文の日本語訳を完成させましょう。

what	何	who	誰	how	どのように
where	どこへ（で）	why	なぜ	how far	どれくらいの距離
when	いつ	which	どれ	how long	どれくらいの時間

Excuse me. <u>Where</u> is the boarding gate for this flight?

( )

<u>How long</u> is the flight to Los Angeles?

( )

be 動詞は、単に「（～は）…である」と言う場合だけでなく、《be going to ...》の形で未来表現、《be + -ing》の形で進行形、《be + 過去分詞》の形で受動態など、様々な表現で使われます。基本をしっかりと確認しておきましょう。

 Let's Listen!　　　　　　　会話の大意を聞き取ろう！

タカシと係員の会話を聞いて、質問に対する答えとして最も適切なものを (A) ～ (C) の中から１つ選びましょう。 1-03

Question 1　What does Takashi give to the officer?

(A) Only his passport

(B) His passport and landing card

(C) His passport, boarding ticket and landing card

Question 2　How long is Takashi going to stay in America?

(A) About a month

(B) Eight weeks

(C) Four months

Question 3　What does Takashi tell the officer?

(A) The address of his hotel

(B) The host family's address

(C) His family name

Let's Check & Read Aloud!   音読してみよう！

1. スクリプトを見ながら会話をもう１度聞き、下線部に当てはまる表現を書き入れましょう。（下線部には単語が２つ入ります） 1-03
2. 内容を確認して、全文を音読してみましょう。
3. タカシと係員の役割をパートナーと一緒に演じてみましょう。

Let's Practice the Roleplay!

Officer's Role   Takashi's Role

最後にQRコードから動画にアクセスして
各自ロールプレイの練習をしましょう。

An officer speaks to Takashi at immigration.

Officer | May I see your passport and landing card, please?

Takashi | Yes, here they are.

Officer | Thank you. Is this your ①＿＿＿＿＿＿＿＿＿ to America?

Takashi | Yes, actually this is my first ②＿＿＿＿＿＿＿＿＿ .

Officer | What's ③＿＿＿＿＿＿＿＿＿ of your visit?

Takashi | Sightseeing.

Officer | ④＿＿＿＿＿＿＿＿＿ traveling alone?

Takashi | Yes, I'm traveling alone.

Officer | Uh-huh. ⑤＿＿＿＿＿＿＿＿＿ are you going to stay in America?

Takashi | Four weeks.

Officer | And where will you ⑥＿＿＿＿＿＿＿＿＿ ?

Takashi | I'll be staying with the Reagans. They are my host family.
⑦＿＿＿＿＿＿＿＿＿ at 385 East Mill Street, San Bernardino.

Officer | I see. Have a ⑧＿＿＿＿＿＿＿＿＿ .

Takashi | Thank you.

〰〰 音読のヒント 💡

ウォーキングなど、カタカナ英語の影響もあって、going など動詞の ing 形を「ゴーイング」のように「～イング」と発音する人がいますが、ing の [ɪŋ] における [ŋ] は「ング」という感じの鼻にかけた音で、「グ」の音は鼻から出ていくため、はっきりとは聞こえない音です。「イング」ではなく、「イング」という感じです。他にも、sightseeing を「サイトシーング」のように、「スィ」[si] を「シ」[ʃí] と読んでしまいがちですが、正しく「サイトスィーイング」[sáɪtsìːɪŋ] と発音するように心がけましょう。

A. 例にならい、カッコ内に適切な be 動詞を書き入れましょう。

> 例 Ladies and gentlemen, this (*is*) your captain speaking.

1. This is our first trip abroad, so we (　　　　　) very excited.

2. My mother (　　　　　) a flight attendant, but she's a housewife now.

3. (　　　　　) this the check-in counter for flights to Los Angeles?

4. The airport (　　　　　) closed for two days last week.

B. 例にならい、A と B の対話が成り立つように枠の中から適切な疑問詞を選んで文を完成させましょう。

> 例 A: ___What is___ the purpose of your visit?
> B: Sightseeing.

what ✓
when
who
where
why
how
how long
how much
how far

1. A: _____ the next bus for the airport?

   B: In 20 minutes.

2. A: _____ the Tourist Information Center?

   B: It's on the first floor, near the bank.

3. A: Excuse me, _____ the flight?

   B: It's about 12 hours, sir.

4. A: _____ it between Tokyo and Los Angeles?

   B: About 8,800 kilometers.

C. 日本語の意味に合うようにカッコ内の語句を並べ替え、英文を完成させましょう。ただし、文の始めにくる単語も小文字にしてあり、<u>1 つ余分な語句が含まれています</u>。

1. 空港は非常に混雑していました。

   (was / are / the / crowded / airport / very).

   _____

2. 機内後部には空席がいくつかあります。

   (are / vacant seats / in / some / is / there) the rear of the cabin.

   _____

3. どうしてあなたの便は遅れたのですか？

   (delayed / were / was / flight / why / your)?

   _____

4. 両替所は何階にありますか？

   On (is / exchange counter / floor / what / the / are)?

   _____

 **Let's Read!**　　　　　　　　　　　　　　　　　　　　読解力を高めよう！

次のパッセージを読み、その内容について１〜３の質問に答えましょう。　　 1-04

How to Prepare for Your Homestay

If you're planning to study abroad, there are many ways to prepare for your trip. First, you should research the places you're going to visit. You can begin by taking a look at your school and homestay neighborhood on Google Earth. You can also practice explaining your culture and everyday life. It's a good idea to prepare photos of your school life, your family, and your house. Showing photos to your homestay family will make communication easier for you. And try to contact your host family by e-mail before you arrive. This will help you to build a good relationship.

1. If you're planning to study abroad, you can research your destination by ＿＿＿＿＿.

    (A) explaining your culture

    (B) contacting your homestay neighborhood

    (C) using Google Earth

2. Preparing photos of your everyday life will ＿＿＿＿＿.

    (A) make it easier to talk to your hosts

    (B) often fail to build a good relationship

    (C) cause problems at the airport

3. Sending your host family an e-mail ＿＿＿＿＿.

    (A) should only be done after you arrive

    (B) is a good way to get to know them

    (C) is not a very good idea

 [Notes]

research: 調査する　　neighborhood: 近所　　relationship: 関係

Challenge Yourself! リスニング力を試そう！

Part I PHOTOGRAPHS

(A)～(C) の英文を聞き、写真の描写として最も適切なものを選びましょう。 1-05

1.

2.

(A)　　(B)　　(C)　　　　　　　(A)　　(B)　　(C)

Part II QUESTION-RESPONSE

最初に聞こえてくる英文に対する応答として最も適切なものを (A)～(C) の中から選びましょう。 1-06

3.　(A)　　(B)　　(C)

4.　(A)　　(B)　　(C)

Part III SHORT CONVERSATIONS

会話を聞き、下の英文が会話の内容と合っていれば T (True)、間違っていれば F (False) を○で囲みましょう。 1-07

5. The woman tells the man to sit down.　　　　　　　　T　　　F

6. The man will be staying in the U.S. for two months.　　T　　　F

 Let's Read Aloud & Write! 音読筆写で覚えよう！

授業のまとめとして、今日学習した対話文を3回書き写してしっかり覚えましょう。1度英文を声に出して読んでから書き写すと頭に残りやすくなります。

今日のまとめ

英語で答えられますか？　　Are you afraid of flying?

UNIT 02 Do you have anything to declare?

文法 一般動詞（現在形）

無事入国審査を終えたタカシは、続いて税関で所持品の検査を受けます。会話では、指示したり、依頼したりする際の表現を学びます。また、文法では**一般動詞（現在形）**に焦点を当てて学習します。

 Warm-up　　　　　　　　　　　　　　授業前に確認しておこう！

≫ *Vocabulary Preview*

1 ～ 10 の語句の意味として適切なものを a ～ j の中から選びましょう。　　🎵 1-08

1. declare	_____	a.	手荷物
2. form	_____	b.	個人の
3. suitcase	_____	c.	みやげ
4. declaration	_____	d.	（複数形で）所有物
5. personal	_____	e.	税関
6. customs	_____	f.	（要求に対する返事として）いいですよ
7. certainly	_____	g.	スーツケース
8. baggage	_____	h.	（税関で）～を申告する
9. belongings	_____	i.	申告
10. souvenir	_____	j.	用紙

ビートに乗って 1 ～ 10 の語句を発音してみましょう。

≫ *Grammar Point :* 一般動詞（現在形）

I'm a flight attendant. I <u>work</u> on a plane.

（私はフライトアテンダントです。機内で働いています）

My brother is an immigration officer. He <u>works</u> at Narita International Airport.

（兄は出入国審査官です。成田国際空港で働いています）

be 動詞以外の動詞を**一般動詞**と呼び、現在の状況や習慣を示す場合、**現在形**を用います。ほとんどの場合、現在形は動詞のもとの形（＝**原形**）と同じですが、主語が 3 人称・単数・現在形の場合には語尾に -s や -es がつきます。下の表の空欄に適切な動詞の形を書き入れて確認しましょう。

1. 多くの動詞	語尾に -s をつける	like → likes	want → wants
2. -s, -sh, -ch, -x, <子音字＋o> で終わる動詞	語尾に -es をつける	go → goes	pass → teach →
3. <子音字＋y> で終わる動詞	y を i に変えて -es をつける	fly → flies	carry →
4. 例外的な動詞	不規則な変化をする	have → has	

> a, i, u, e, o のことを**母音字**、それ以外を**子音字**と言います。

一般動詞を使った現在形の文を疑問文にするときは、文の始めに do を持ってきます。また否定文にするには動詞のすぐ前に don't（=do not）をつけます。主語が 3 人称で単数の場合は doesn't や does を使い、動詞は語尾の -s や -es を外して原形に戻します。下の例文の日本語訳を完成させながら確認しましょう。

> **Do** you often travel abroad?
> (　　　　　　　　　　　　　　　　　　　　　　　　　)
>
> My grandmother **doesn't** like flying. She prefers taking trains.
> (　　　　　　　　　　　　　　　　　　　　　　　　　)

　また、現在形というと現時点だけを示すと考えがちですが、実際には下記の表のように、**現在を中心とした幅広い時間**を示します。**普段のことを話す場合に使う形**と覚えておくとよいでしょう。下の例文の日本語訳を完成させながら確認しましょう。

> 「今〜している」のように、現在の動作を表す場合**現在進行形**（Unit 4）を用います。

現在の状態	I love flying. I feel great. (　　　　　　　　　　)	現在
習慣的な動作	My sister often travels abroad on business. (　　　　　　　　　)	現在
一般的な事実・真理	The sun rises in the east. (　　　　　　　　　)	現在

Let's Listen!

会話の大意を聞き取ろう！

タカシと係員の会話を聞いて、質問に対する答えとして最も適切なものを（A）〜（C）の中から 1 つ選びましょう。

 1-09

Question 1　What does Takashi give to the officer?

(A) Only his passport
(B) His passport and customs declaration form
(C) His passport, boarding ticket and customs declaration form

Question 2　Does Takashi have anything to declare?

(A) Yes, he has one souvenir to declare.
(B) Yes, he has some personal belongings to declare.
(C) No, he doesn't have anything to declare.

Question 3　What does the officer ask Takashi to do?

(A) Open his suitcase
(B) Put his personal belongings on the counter
(C) Fill in the customs declaration form

Let's Check & Read Aloud! 音読してみよう！

1. スクリプトを見ながら会話をもう1度聞き、下線部に当てはまる表現を書き入れ 1-09
   ましょう。（下線部には単語が2つ入ります）
2. 内容を確認して、全文を音読してみましょう。
3. タカシと係員の役割をパートナーと一緒に演じてみましょう。

Let's Practice the Roleplay!

Officer's Role　Takashi's Role

An officer speaks to Takashi at customs.

Officer May I see your passport and customs declaration form?

Takashi Yes, here you go.

Officer Thank you. Please put all ①＿＿＿＿＿＿＿＿ on the counter.

Takashi Sure.

Officer Thank you. Do you have anything ②＿＿＿＿＿＿＿＿ ?

Takashi No, I ③＿＿＿＿＿＿＿＿ so.

Officer ④＿＿＿＿＿＿＿＿ the suitcase?

Takashi Just my ⑤＿＿＿＿＿＿＿＿ .

Officer Could you please ⑥＿＿＿＿＿＿＿＿ just in case?

Takashi Certainly.

Officer ⑦＿＿＿＿＿＿＿＿ these?

Takashi These ⑧＿＿＿＿＿＿＿＿ for my host family.

Officer I see. Enjoy your trip!

Takashi Thanks. I will.

∿∿ 音読のヒント ·ᄷ·

"Thank you." [θǽŋkjù] は非常によく使う表現ですから、カタカナ英語で「サンキュー」とならない
ように、しっかり練習しましょう。th の発音記号 [θ] は前歯で舌の先を軽く噛んだ状態で「スー」っ
と息を吐く音で、カタカナではうまく書き表すことができません。舌を軽く出して素早く引きながら
発音します。「サァンキュゥ」のような感じです。

 ***Grammar*** 文法に強くなろう！

A. 例にならい、枠の中から適切な単語を選び、必要な場合は適切な形にして次の 1 〜 4 の文を完成させましょう。

例 Ben (*speaks*) three languages.

1. Jack is a customs inspector. He (　　　　　) baggage.

2. Where can I (　　　　　) up my baggage?

3. Do you (　　　　　) a return ticket to Japan?

4. How often does the shuttle bus (　　　　　) the airport?

> pick
> leave
> speak ✓
> work
> check
> have

B. 例にならい、カッコ内の動詞を肯定・否定・疑問のいずれか適切な形に変えて文を完成させましょう。2 は主語として you を補いましょう。

例 My father often travels on business, but he _doesn't enjoy_ it. (enjoy)

1. Hurry! We _____ much time. (have)

2. "_____ any luggage to check?" "Yes, I have one suitcase." (have)

3. "What time does boarding start?" "Boarding _____ at 9:30 at gate 12." (start)

4. Excuse me, but I think you _____ in my seat. (be)

C. 日本語の意味に合うようにカッコ内の語句を並べ替え、英文を完成させましょう。ただし、文の始めにくる単語も小文字にしてあり、1 つ余分な語句が含まれています。

1. 申告するものは何もありません。

(have / don't / nothing / declare / to / I).

_____

2. このバスは何分おきに出ますか？

(do / often / this bus / how / run / does)?

_____

3. 父は毎月海外に出かけます。

(go / goes / every / father / my / abroad) month.

_____

4. この搭乗口にどうやって行けばいいですか？

(am / do / how / to / get / I) this gate?

_____

 **Let's Read!**

次のパッセージを読み、その内容について 1 ～ 3 の質問に答えましょう。 1-10

Airline Baggage Rules

These days, airport security will check your baggage very carefully. They'll ask you, "Do you have any dangerous items in your bags?" "Did you pack your bags by yourself?" Remember, scissors, knives and other dangerous items aren't allowed in your hand baggage. Containers with liquids, gels or creams over 100 ml aren't, either. Also, be careful with fruit and vegetables. Some countries don't allow you to import fresh fruit or vegetables. Finally, be careful that your suitcase isn't too heavy. The limit on most economy class flights is 20-23 kg. If you pay for <u>excess</u> baggage, it can become very expensive!

---

1. At airport security, you will be asked if _____.

   (A) you have seen any dangerous people

   (B) you packed your own bags

   (C) your suitcase is too heavy

2. _____ are allowed in your hand baggage.

   (A) Scissors

   (B) Containers with liquids more than 100 ml

   (C) Containers with gels less than 100 ml

3. The underlined word "excess" means _____ the permitted limit.

   (A) over

   (B) below

   (C) close to

 [Notes]

item: 品物　　　container: 容器　　　gel: ジェル（ゼリー状の整髪料）
underlined: 下線が引かれた

Challenge Yourself!

(A)〜(C) の英文を聞き、写真の描写として最も適切なものを選びましょう。 1-11

1.

    (A)   (B)   (C)

2.

    (A)   (B)   (C)

Part II QUESTION-RESPONSE

最初に聞こえてくる英文に対する応答として最も適切なものを (A)〜(C) の中から選びましょう。 1-12

  3. (A)   (B)   (C)

  4. (A)   (B)   (C)

Part III SHORT CONVERSATIONS

会話を聞き、下の英文が会話の内容と合っていれば T（True）、間違っていれば F（False）を○で囲みましょう。 1-13

  5. The man's carry-on baggage is too heavy.   T   F

  6. The woman is waiting for her baggage in the wrong place.   T   F

 Let's Read Aloud & Write!

音読筆写で覚えよう！

授業のまとめとして、今日学習した対話文を 3 回書き写してしっかり覚えましょう。1 度英文を声に出して読んでから書き写すと頭に残りやすくなります。

今日のまとめ

英語で答えられますか？   Do you like to travel?

文法 一般動詞（過去形）

ホストファミリーのドナが、税関検査を終えたタカシを到着ロビーで出迎えます。会話では、自己紹介したり、感謝したりする際の表現を学びます。また、文法では一般動詞（過去形）に焦点を当てて学習します。

 Warm-up 　　　　　　　　　　　　　授業前に確認しておこう！

≫ Vocabulary Preview

1 ～ 10 の語句の意味として適切なものを a ～ j の中から選びましょう。　　　🎧 1-14

1. view	_____	a. ～を出迎える
2. tired	_____	b. 駐車場
3. arrival	_____	c. 実際には、本当に
4. amazing	_____	d. 景色
5. excited	_____	e. 興奮した
6. must	_____	f. 疲れて
7. meet	_____	g. ～について述べる
8. parking lot	_____	h. ～に違いない
9. really	_____	i. 素晴らしい、驚くほどの
10. mention	_____	j. 到着

ビートに乗って 1 ～ 10 の語句を発音してみましょう。

≫ Grammar Point : 一般動詞（過去形）

I <u>enjoyed</u> the latest movies on the plane. 　　（私は機内で最新の映画を楽しみました）

My parents <u>came</u> to the airport to see me off. 　　（両親が空港に見送りに来てくれました）

　過去の状況や行為・出来事を示す場合、**過去形**を用います。一般動詞を過去形にする場合には語尾に -ed をつけます。ただし、不規則に変化するものも多いので注意が必要です。巻末資料を参考にしながら下の表の空欄に適切な動詞の過去形を書き入れ確認しましょう。

1. ほとんどの動詞		語尾に -ed をつける	help → helped	listen → listened
2. -e で終わる動詞		語尾に -d をつける	use → used	like →
3. y で終わる動詞	母音字＋y の場合	語尾に -ed をつける	enjoy → enjoyed	play →
	子音字＋y の場合	y を i に変えて -ed をつける	study → studied	carry →
4. 母音字 1 つ＋子音字 1 つで終わる動詞*		語尾の子音を重ねて -ed をつける	plan → planned	stop →
5. 例外的な動詞		不規則な変化をする	have → had	write →

＊厳密には、visit や remember、listen のように、最後の音節が強く発音されないものは子音字を重ねません。

一般動詞を使った過去形の文を否定文にするときは、動詞のすぐ前に didn't（=did not）をつけます。また疑問文にするには文の始めに did を持ってきます。いずれの場合も動詞は原形に戻します。下の例文の日本語訳を完成させながら確認しましょう。

Did you have a good sleep on the plane?
(　　　　　　　　　　　　　　　　　　　　　　)

No, I **didn't** get any sleep.
(　　　　　　　　　　　　　　　　　　　　　　)

また、過去形で表される内容は、下記の表や図のように、現在とはつながりがないのがポイントです。下の例文の日本語訳を完成させながら確認しましょう。

過去の状態	I wanted to become a pilot when I was little. (　　　　　　　　　　　　)	過去　　現在
過去の1回きりの行為・出来事	My family went on a trip to Hawaii last summer. (　　　　　　　　　　　　)	過去　　現在
過去の習慣や反復的行為	My father often went abroad on business. (　　　　　　　　　　　　)	過去　　現在

「その時～していた」のように、過去に一時的に続いていた
行為を表す場合は**過去進行形**（Unit 4）を用います。

 Let's Listen!　　　　　　　　　　会話の大意を聞き取ろう！

タカシとドナの会話を聞いて、質問に対する答えとして最も適切なものを（A）～（C） 1-15
の中から１つ選びましょう。

Question 1　What did Takashi do during the flight?

(A) He enjoyed watching movies.
(B) He enjoyed the view from the window.
(C) He slept most of the time.

Question 2　How is Takashi feeling now?

(A) Very tired
(B) Very relaxed
(C) Very excited

Question 3　What does Donna offer to do?

(A) Carry his luggage
(B) Buy him lunch
(C) Take him to the bus stop

Let's Check & Read Aloud!　音読してみよう！

1. スクリプトを見ながら会話をもう1度聞き、下線部に当てはまる表現を書き入れ 1-15
   ましょう。（下線部には単語が2つ入ります）
2. 内容を確認して、全文を音読してみましょう。
3. タカシとドナの役割をパートナーと一緒に演じてみましょう。

Let's Practice the Roleplay!

Donna's Role　Takashi's Role

Donna speaks to Takashi at the arrivals gate.

Donna　Hello, you ①_____ Takashi. Welcome to America.
Nice to meet you.

Takashi　Nice to meet you too, Mrs. Reagan. Thank you very much for
②_____ at the airport. I hope it wasn't a long wait.

Donna　Don't ③_____ . And just call me Donna, OK?
So, ④_____ your flight?

Takashi　It was long, but I enjoyed the view from the plane. It ⑤_____ !

Donna　I see. How long was the flight to Los Angeles?

Takashi　About 10 hours.

Donna　You must ⑥_____ .

Takashi　Not really. This is my first visit to the United States, so I'm very excited.

Donna　That's good. My car ⑦_____ in the parking lot. Can I help you
with the suitcase?

Takashi　Oh thanks, but it's OK. I'll carry ⑧_____ .

♒♒音読のヒント 💡

「子音で終わる単語」の後に「母音で始まる単語」が続いた場合には、単語と単語がつながって聞こ
えることがあります。これを音の連結と言い、例えばcan I は「キャン・アイ」ではなく「キャナイ」
のように聞こえます。音読する際は、モデル音声のように連結させて読むべきところは連結させて音
読し、カタカナ英語の発音にならないようにしましょう。

A. 例にならい、枠の中から適切な単語を選び、必要な場合は適切な形にして次の 1 ～ 4 の文を完成させましょう。

例　My parents (*came*) to the airport to see me off.

| come ✓ |
| sleep |
| go |
| pick |
| have |

1. I checked in my bags and (　　　　　) to security.

2. Donna (　　　　　) me up at the airport yesterday.

3. Did you (　　　　) a good flight?

4. I (　　　　) for only three hours so I could catch the first train.

B. 例にならい、カッコ内の動詞を肯定・否定・疑問のいずれか適切な形に変えて文を完成させましょう。2 は主語として you を補いましょう。

例　It was very noisy outside, so I <u>*didn't get*</u> any sleep last night. (get)

1. The suitcase was too expensive, so I ＿＿＿＿＿＿＿＿＿ it. (buy)

2. "＿＿＿＿＿＿＿＿＿ a bus from the airport?" "No, Donna gave me a ride." (take)

3. I didn't sleep well last night. I ＿＿＿＿＿＿＿＿＿ up in the middle of the night. (wake)

4. I watched a film on the plane, but I ＿＿＿＿＿＿＿＿＿ asleep watching it. (fall)

C. 日本語の意味に合うようにカッコ内の語句を並べ替え、英文を完成させましょう。ただし、文の始めにくる単語も小文字にしてあり、<u>1 つ余分な語句が含まれています</u>。

1. 機内ではよく眠れました。

(had / a / was / sleep / I / good) on the plane.

＿＿＿＿＿＿＿＿＿＿＿＿＿＿＿＿＿＿＿＿＿＿＿＿＿＿＿

2. 入国審査ではまったく苦労しませんでした。

(have / any / didn't / had / trouble / I) at immigration.

＿＿＿＿＿＿＿＿＿＿＿＿＿＿＿＿＿＿＿＿＿＿＿＿＿＿＿

3. 彼は羽田空港から（飛行機に）乗ったのですか？

(did / was / from / he / Haneda / fly) Airport?

＿＿＿＿＿＿＿＿＿＿＿＿＿＿＿＿＿＿＿＿＿＿＿＿＿＿＿

4. スーツケースは何個預けたのですか？

(were / suitcases / did / you / how / many) check in?

＿＿＿＿＿＿＿＿＿＿＿＿＿＿＿＿＿＿＿＿＿＿＿＿＿＿＿

 **Let's Read!**

次のパッセージを読み、その内容について 1 〜 3 の質問に答えましょう。 1-16

An Unfamiliar House

Homestay life won't be the same as in your own home. For example, when you do laundry in a homestay, the washing machine may be in the kitchen, or even in the garage. In some countries the weather isn't so good, so many people prefer to dry their clothes in a dryer. In Japan, bathrooms are usually downstairs, ⬚ in many countries, the bathroom will be upstairs, and many homestays will have more than one. If you're lucky, your bedroom may have a <u>private</u> bathroom. Also, in some countries the toilet will be *in* the bathroom. Differences like these make cultural exchange more interesting!

1. The word that belongs in the ⬚ in this passage is _____.

   (A) because

   (B) but

   (C) so

2. The underlined word "private" means _____.

   (A) secret

   (B) expensive

   (C) your own

3. You _____ your homestay life to be the same as your home life.

   (A) shouldn't expect

   (B) can expect

   (C) must ask for

 [Notes]

bathroom: バスルーム（浴槽、シャワー、洗面台があり、アメリカでは右写真のように通常トイレも付く）

toilet:《主に英》トイレ（もともとの意味は「便器」で、アメリカではトイレの意味では toilet ではなく bathroom を使う）

the word that belongs in the ⬚ : 空欄にあてはまる単語

Challenge Yourself! リスニング力を試そう！

Part I PHOTOGRAPHS

(A)～(C) の英文を聞き、写真の描写として最も適切なものを選びましょう。 1-17

1.

     (A)   (B)   (C)

2.

     (A)   (B)   (C)

Part II QUESTION-RESPONSE

最初に聞こえてくる英文に対する応答として最も適切なものを (A)～(C) の中から選びましょう。 1-18

  3. (A)   (B)   (C)

  4. (A)   (B)   (C)

Part III SHORT CONVERSATIONS

会話を聞き、下の英文が会話の内容と合っていれば T (True)、間違っていれば F (False) を○で囲みましょう。 1-19

  5. It's 10 o'clock in Japan now.   T   F

  6. The man went to bed at three a.m.   T   F

 Let's Read Aloud & Write! 音読筆写で覚えよう！

授業のまとめとして、今日学習した対話文を 3 回書き写してしっかり覚えましょう。1 度英文を声に出して読んでから書き写すと頭に残りやすくなります。

今日のまとめ

英語で答えられますか？   Did you sleep well last night?

UNIT 04 Are you still feeling tired?

文法 進行形

いよいよホストファミリーとの生活が始まり、キッチンでドナがタカシに話しかけます。会話では、提案したり、許可を求めたりする際の表現を学びます。また、文法では**進行形**に焦点を当てて学習します。

Warm-up

授業前に確認しておこう！

≫ Vocabulary Preview

1～10 の語句の意味として適切なものを a～j の中から選びましょう。

🎵 1-20

1. suffer from	＿＿＿	a.	時差ぼけ
2. journey	＿＿＿	b.	寝つく
3. clothes	＿＿＿	c.	提案する
4. still	＿＿＿	d.	洗濯物
5. suggest	＿＿＿	e.	どういうわけか
6. sleepy	＿＿＿	f.	～に苦しむ
7. jet lag	＿＿＿	g.	旅行
8. fall asleep	＿＿＿	h.	今でもまだ
9. laundry	＿＿＿	i.	眠い
10. somehow	＿＿＿	j.	衣類

ビートに乗って 1～10 の語句を発音してみましょう。

≫ Grammar Point : 進行形

I <u>travel</u> abroad every summer. （私は毎年夏に海外旅行をします）〔現在形〕
I'<u>m traveling</u> abroad right now. （私は今海外旅行中です）〔現在進行形〕
I <u>was traveling</u> abroad at that time. （私はそのとき海外旅行中でした）〔過去進行形〕

　一般に現在形が普段の状態や動作を指すのに対し、今している最中の動作を表す場合には**現在進行形**を用い、≪ be 動詞＋動詞の ing 形≫の形で表します。下の表の空欄に適切な動詞の形を書き入れて動詞の ing 形の作り方を確認しましょう。

1. ほとんどの動詞	語尾に ing をつける	sleep → sleeping	eat → *eating*
2. 子音＋ -e で終わる動詞	語尾の e を取って ing をつける	give → giving	make →
3. -ie [ai] で終わる動詞	語尾の ie を y に変えて ing をつける	lie → lying	die →
4. 1 母音字＋1 子音字で終わる動詞	語尾の子音字を重ねて ing をつける	get → getting	stop →

過去形の be 動詞を使って**過去進行形**にすると「〜していた」という意味を表します。また、否定文にするときはbe動詞のすぐ後にnotをつけ、疑問文にするにはbe動詞を主語の前に持ってきます。下の例文の日本語訳を完成させながら使い方を確認しましょう。

I called you three times. What were you doing?
Were you sleeping?
(   )

Sorry. I wasn't sleeping. I was taking a shower.
(   )

進行形は「〜している」のように動作を表すものですから、know（知っている）などのように状態を表す動詞は通常、進行形にはなりません。ただし、have や live のように状態を表す動詞でも、次のような場合は進行形にすることができます。

We're having a good time.　　　　　　　　　　　　（私たちは楽しんでいる最中です）

　　　　　　　　　　　　　　　　　　＊この have は「（時などを）過ごす」という意味

My father is living in New York on business.　　（父は仕事でニューヨークに住んでいます）

　　　　　＊ live は一般に「住んでいる」という状態を表しますが、進行形にすると「ずっとそこに
　　　　　　住むわけではなく、一時的に住んでいる」という意味になります。

 Let's Listen!　　　　　　　　　　会話の大意を聞き取ろう！

タカシとドナの会話を聞いて、質問に対する答えとして最も適切なものを(A)〜(C)　 1-21
の中から1つ選びましょう。

Question 1　　How is Takashi feeling now?

(A) Tired but excited
(B) Sleepy and tired
(C) Sick and tired

Question 2　　What does Donna suggest?

(A) That he should go to bed
(B) That he should wash his clothes
(C) That he should take a shower

Question 3　　What does Takashi ask Donna?

(A) When he should do his laundry
(B) When he should take a shower
(C) How to use the washing machine

Let's Check & Read Aloud!

音読してみよう！

1. スクリプトを見ながら会話をもう1度聞き、下線部に当てはまる表現を書き入れ 1-21
   ましょう。（下線部には単語が2つ入ります）
2. 内容を確認して、全文を音読してみましょう。
3. タカシとドナの役割をパートナーと一緒に演じてみましょう。

Let's Practice the Roleplay!

Donna's Role   Takashi's Role

Donna speaks to Takashi in the kitchen.

Donna	Good morning, Takashi. How are you? Did you sleep well?
Takashi	Morning, Donna. I'm fine, but I didn't sleep well last night. Even though I was tired after the ①_____ , I somehow couldn't ②_____ .
Donna	That's too bad. Well, I think ③_____ from jet lag. Are you still feeling tired?
Takashi	Yes, I'm feeling tired and sleepy.
Donna	④_____ you take a shower?
Takashi	That's a good idea. Oh, can I ask you a question? I ⑤_____ wash my clothes. When would be a ⑥_____ for me to do laundry?
Donna	Any time is fine.
Takashi	Thanks. Is it OK if I do it after I take a shower?
Donna	Of course. ⑦_____ show you where everything is. Here, this is the ⑧_____ , and this is the dryer. If you need anything, just ask.
Takashi	I will, thank you.

♒ 音読のヒント 💡

単語の最後にくる l [l] は、つづり字からつい「ル」に近い音を予想しますが、実際には「ゥ」のように聞こえます。例えば、well [wél] は「ウェル」ではなく、むしろ「ウェゥ」のように聞こえます。well は、「上手に、十分に」という副詞だけでなく、「ええと、そうですね、さて」という間投詞としても使われますが、この場合は話のつなぎということを意識して発音すると良いでしょう。

Grammar   文法に強くなろう！

A. 例にならい、枠の中から適切な単語を選び、必要な場合は適切な形にして次の１〜４の文を完成させましょう。

> 例 It (*is raining*). Take an umbrella.

know
rain ✓
snow
take
wait

1. Let's hurry. Everyone (　　　　　) for us.

2. Donna (　　　　　) a shower every morning.

3. It (　　　　　) when I got up this morning.

4. I (　　　　　) Ron's phone number. Shall I call him?

B. 例にならい、次の英文をカッコ内の指示に従って書き換えましょう。

> 例 Ron reads the newspaper.（現在進行形に）　　*Ron is reading the newspaper.*

1. Beth doesn't use a computer.（現在進行形に）

　　_____

2. We had a good time at the party.（過去進行形に）

　　_____

3. Do you suffer from jet lag?（現在進行形に）

　　_____

4. Did you use the washing machine?（過去進行形に）

　　_____

C. 日本語の意味に合うようにカッコ内の語句を並べ替え、英文を完成させましょう。ただし、文の始めにくる単語も小文字にしてあり、１つ余分な語句が含まれています。

1. 時差ぼけを感じていますか？

　　(feeling / jet lag / do / you / any / are)?

　　_____

2. その時はシャワーを浴びていました。

　　I (taking / at / a shower / that time / was / am).

　　_____

3. 時差ぼけについてはよく知っています。

　　(a lot / jet lag / I / know / am knowing / about).

　　_____

4. ロンはいつ帰って来る予定ですか？

　　(coming / when / is / come / back / Ron)?

　　_____

 **Let's Read!**

次のパッセージを読み、その内容について１〜３の質問に答えましょう。 1-22

Jet Lag and How to Cope with It

Traveling is exciting, but can be tiring, too. If you're flying across time zones, you'll probably suffer from jet lag. Here are some <u>tips</u> to help you overcome travel-related tiredness. First, change your watch to local time as soon as you arrive. If you're going to arrive at night, try to sleep on the plane. If you arrive in daylight, try to enjoy some sunshine. Some light exercise will help you to reset your body clock. Finally, rest well before your trip. Drink plenty of water, and avoid alcohol, coffee and sleeping pills—they make jet lag worse, not better! Bon voyage!

---

1. The underlined word "tips" means _____.

   (A) requests

   (B) goods

   (C) pieces of advice

2. Doing some light daytime exercise _____.

   (A) helps you to overcome jet lag

   (B) makes you feel sleepy

   (C) makes your jet lag worse

3. Which sentence is true?

   (A) Drinking lots of coffee will make your jet lag better.

   (B) Taking sleeping pills will make your jet lag worse.

   (C) You shouldn't drink water at all before your trip.

 [Notes]

tiring: 疲れさせる　　across time zones: 時差を超えて
overcome: 〜を克服する　　Bon voyage!: （仏語）良い旅を！

Challenge Yourself!

Part I PHOTOGRAPHS

(A)〜(C) の英文を聞き、写真の描写として最も適切なものを選びましょう。 1-23

1.

(A)　　　(B)　　　(C)

2.

(A)　　　(B)　　　(C)

Part II QUESTION-RESPONSE

最初に聞こえてくる英文に対する応答として最も適切なものを（A)〜(C) の中から選びましょう。 1-24

3.　(A)　　　(B)　　　(C)

4.　(A)　　　(B)　　　(C)

Part III SHORT CONVERSATIONS

会話を聞き、下の英文が会話の内容と合っていれば T (True)、間違っていれば F (False) を○で囲みましょう。 1-25

5. The woman tells the man that his laundry will be dry by tonight.　　　T　　　F

6. The man prefers to take a shower at night.　　　T　　　F

 Let's Read Aloud & Write! 音読筆写で覚えよう！

授業のまとめとして、今日学習した対話文を3回書き写してしっかり覚えましょう。1度英文を声に出して読んでから書き写すと頭に残りやすくなります。

今日のまとめ

英語で答えられますか？　　　Are you enjoying your English class?

UNIT 05

What are we going to do in the afternoon?

文法 未来表現

英語研修の初日、タカシは教室でベス先生にオリ
エンテーションの内容について尋ねます。会話で
は、予定を述べたり、詳細を尋ねたりする際の表
現を学びます。また、文法では**未来表現**に焦点を
当てて学習します。

Warm-up

授業前に確認しておこう！

≫ Vocabulary Preview

1 ～ 10 の語句の意味として適切なものを a ～ j の中から選びましょう。　　🎵 1-26

1. schedule　　＿＿＿＿＿　　a. 詳細
2. section　　＿＿＿＿＿　　b. ～を説明する
3. recess　　＿＿＿＿＿　　c. 部分
4. show ... around　　＿＿＿＿＿　　d. （仕事などを）一休みする
5. activity　　＿＿＿＿＿　　e. 予定
6. tour　　＿＿＿＿＿　　f. ～を案内する
7. detail　　＿＿＿＿＿　　g. 休憩（時間）
8. placement　　＿＿＿＿＿　　h. 見学
9. break (v.)　　＿＿＿＿＿　　i. 活動
10. explain　　＿＿＿＿＿　　j. クラス分け

[Note] v.: = verb （動詞）

ビートに乗って 1 ～ 10 の語句を発音してみましょう。

≫ Grammar Point : 未来表現

Good morning, everyone. I'll take attendance now.

（みなさん、おはよう。今から出席を取ります）

First, I'm going to talk about the placement test.

（まず、クラス分けテストについてお話します）

　これから先のことを話す場合には、≪ will ＋ 動詞の原形≫や≪ be going to ＋ 動詞の原形≫といっ
た形を使います。下の表で確認しましょう。

will	意志（～するつもりだ）	I'll explain the schedule for today.
	予測（～だろう）	Hurry up, or we'll be late for the orientation.
be going to	計画や意志（～するつもりだ）	I'm going to show you around the campus.
	予測（～だろう）	It's already nine o'clock! We're going to be late for class.

否定文にするときは、≪ will not ＋動詞の原形≫や≪ be not going to ＋動詞の原形≫のように、will や be 動詞のすぐ後に not をつけます。また、疑問文にするには will や be 動詞を主語の前に持ってきます。下の例文の日本語訳を完成させながら確認しましょう。

won't = will not

I'm sorry I was late on my first day. It <u>won't</u> happen again.

(   )

What time <u>will</u> the campus tour start?　(   )

What <u>are</u> you <u>going to</u> do after school?　(   )

will と be going to はどちらもこれから先のことを表しますが、まったく同じ意味というわけではありません。**will は話をしている時点でそうすると決めたことを表す**のに対し、**be going to はすでに以前からそのつもりでいたことを表します。**次の例文でその違いを確認しておきましょう。

"I'd like to know the results of my placement test."
（クラス分けテストの結果を知りたいのですが）

"Sure. Visit my office and I'<u>ll</u> let you know."
（いいですよ。私の研究室を訪ねてくれればお知らせします）

"Can I visit your office after class?"
（授業の後、先生の研究室を訪ねてもよいですか？）

"Sorry. I'<u>m going to</u> be in a meeting at that time. How about tomorrow?"
（ごめんなさい。その時間は会議の予定です。明日はどうですか？）

 Let's Listen!　　　　会話の大意を聞き取ろう！

タカシとベス先生の会話を聞いて、質問に対する答えとして最も適切なものを
(A) 〜 (C) の中から1つ選びましょう。　　 1-27

Question 1　What is true of the placement test?

(A) It's an interview test.

(B) It has four sections.

(C) It takes about an hour.

Question 2　Who will explain about the school activities?

(A) Beth

(B) Martha

(C) Beth and Martha

Question 3　Will Takashi have a campus tour?

(A) Yes, and the tour starts at three.

(B) Yes, and Martha will be conducting it.

(C) No, he won't.

Let's Check & Read Aloud! 音読してみよう！

1. スクリプトを見ながら会話をもう 1 度聞き、下線部に当てはまる表現を書き入れましょう。（下線部には単語が 2 つ入ります） 1-27

2. 内容を確認して、全文を音読してみましょう。

3. タカシとベスの役割をパートナーと一緒に演じてみましょう。

Let's Practice the Roleplay!

Takashi's Role   Beth's Role

Takashi speaks to his English teacher,
Beth in the classroom.

| Takashi | Excuse me, could you tell me the schedule for today? |

| Beth | Sure. First, ①＿＿＿＿＿＿＿＿＿ the placement test. |

| Takashi | OK. What's the test like? |

| Beth | It's a multiple-choice test, and has ②＿＿＿＿＿＿＿＿＿ : listening, grammar, and reading. |

| Takashi | How long does it take? |

| Beth | It ③＿＿＿＿＿＿＿＿ 60 minutes. Then ④＿＿＿＿＿＿＿＿＿ for lunch. You have to come back here at one o'clock. |

| Takashi | All right. What are we ⑤＿＿＿＿＿＿＿ do after the recess? |

| Beth | ⑥＿＿＿＿＿＿＿＿＿ the English program in detail and Martha will talk to you about the school activities and services. |

| Takashi | Do we have a campus tour? |

| Beth | Of course. Martha will show ⑦＿＿＿＿＿＿＿＿ the campus after her talk. ⑧＿＿＿＿＿＿＿＿ the orientation by three o'clock. |

♒ 音読のヒント ☀

the English program の the をつい「ザ」[ðə] と言ってしまうかもしれませんが、母音で始まる単語の前にある the は「ジ」[ði] と発音します。ただし、unit のように、母音字 u で始まっていても実際の発音が母音で始まらない場合は「ザ」と発音します。

例：the university [ðə jùːnəvə́ːrsəti]

また、listening, grammar, and reading の前にある「：」はコロンといい、例示する前などに使われます。音読する際は、コロンの後で一息置くと良いでしょう。

A. 例にならい枠の中から適切な単語を選び、必要な場合は適切な形にして次の 1 ～ 4 の文を完成
させましょう。

> 例　It's Takashi's birthday tomorrow. He'll (　*be*　) 20.

> 1.　"Are you coming with me?"　"No, I'll (　　　　　) here."
>
> 2.　Don't worry about the test. You'll (　　　　　) an A.
>
> 3.　Beth is going to (　　　　　) you about the program in detail.
>
> 4.　Let's wait here until everyone (　　　　　) back from the campus tour.

| be ✓ |
| come |
| get |
| stay |
| tell |

B. 例にならい、カッコ内から正しい語句を選び○で囲みましょう。

> 例　Hurry! It's already nine o'clock. (　We won't　/ We're going to) be late.

> 1.　"Are you ready?"　"Not yet, but (I'll / I won't) be ready in 10 minutes.
>
> 2.　"Is Yoona coming to the party?"　"I don't know. (I'll / I'm going to) ask her."
>
> 3.　I'm worried about the test. If I don't get over 60 percent, I (won't / will) pass.
>
> 4.　"How about going out for dinner?"　"Sorry. (I'll / I'm going to) go to a concert tonight."

C. 日本語の意味に合うようにカッコ内の語句を並べ替え、英文を完成させましょう。ただし、文
の始めにくる単語も小文字にしてあり、<u>1 つ余分な語句が含まれています</u>。

> 1.　キャンパスツアーの後は何をする予定ですか？
>
> (are / will / what / to do / we / going) after the campus tour?
>
> _____
>
> 2.　キャンパスツアーの後で歓迎会を行います。
>
> (welcome / we're / we'll / a / party / having) after the campus tour.
>
> _____
>
> 3.　10 分を超える遅刻は欠席と見なします。
>
> If you're more than 10 minutes late,(consider / won't / absence / an / it / I'll).
>
> _____
>
> 4.　後でキャンパスを案内します。
>
> (you / I'll / I'm going / the campus / around / show) later.
>
> _____

 **Let's Read!**

読解力を高めよう！

次のパッセージを読み、その内容について１〜３の質問に答えましょう。 🎧 1-28

The House Rules

Host families often have house rules for homestay students. For example, many families try to save energy, so turn off the light when you go out. Many areas suffer from water shortages, so take a short shower, ☐ a long bath. Most families want you to tell them in advance if you're going to miss a meal, or invite friends to the house. One useful piece of advice is that, if you break or damage anything, don't try to hide it. Tell your host family as soon as possible, and offer to pay for the thing you damaged. Honesty is the best policy!

---

1. The phrase that belongs in the ☐ in this passage is _____.

   (A) for example

   (B) because of

   (C) instead of

2. If you're going to miss a meal, you should _____ beforehand.

   (A) take a short shower

   (B) tell your host mother

   (C) invite friends to the house

3. If you break or damage anything at your host family's house, you should _____.

   (A) tell your host family first

   (B) buy a new one as soon as possible

   (C) offer to repair it by yourself

 [Notes]

shortage: 不足　　　in advance: 前もって　　　honesty: 正直　　　policy: 方策

Challenge Yourself! リスニング力を試そう！

Part I PHOTOGRAPHS

(A)〜(C) の英文を聞き、写真の描写として最も適切なものを選びましょう。 1-29

1.

(A)　　　(B)　　　(C)

2.

(A)　　　(B)　　　(C)

Part II QUESTION-RESPONSE

最初に聞こえてくる英文に対する応答として最も適切なものを（A)〜(C) の中から選びましょう。 1-30

3.　(A)　　　(B)　　　(C)

4.　(A)　　　(B)　　　(C)

Part III SHORT CONVERSATIONS

会話を聞き、下の英文が会話の内容と合っていれば T（True)、間違っていれば F（False) を○で囲みましょう。 1-31

5. The man is looking forward to the library orientation.　　　T　　　F

6. The i-zone closes at eight in the evening.　　　T　　　F

 Let's Read Aloud & Write! 音読筆写で覚えよう！

授業のまとめとして、今日学習した対話文を3回書き写してしっかり覚えましょう。1度英文を声に出して読んでから書き写すと頭に残りやすくなります。

今日のまとめ

英語で答えられますか？　　　What are you going to do this weekend?

It's called Mountain Grove.

 文法 受動態

初日の英語研修から帰宅したタカシはリビングルームでドナと学校の話をしています。会話では、様子を尋ねたり、あいづちを打ったりする際の表現を学びます。また、文法では**受動態**に焦点を当てて学習します。

Warm-up

授業前に確認しておこう！

≫ *Vocabulary Preview*

1 ～ 10 の語句の意味として適切なものを a ～ j の中から選びましょう。　　CD 1-32

1. sound	＿＿＿＿	a. 同じ
2. nearby	＿＿＿＿	b. ショッピングセンター
3. both	＿＿＿＿	c. ～の辺りに
4. same	＿＿＿＿	d. 近くの、近くに
5. shopping mall	＿＿＿＿	e. （車で行く）道のり
6. stationery	＿＿＿＿	f. 残業する
7. around	＿＿＿＿	g. ～を閉める
8. work late	＿＿＿＿	h. ～に思える、～に聞こえる
9. drive	＿＿＿＿	i. 文房具
10. close（v.）	＿＿＿＿	j. 両方とも

ビートに乗って 1 ～ 10 の語句を発音してみましょう。

≫ *Grammar Point :* 受動態

Ron cleaned the living room.

（ロンがリビングルームの掃除をしました）〔能動態〕

The living room was cleaned by Ron.

（リビングルームの掃除はロンによってされました）〔受動態〕

「～によって」は by で表しますが、誰がしたのかが重要でない場合には不要です。

　「～は…される／されている」のように、何らかの動作を受ける意味を表す場合には、**受動態**を用い、≪ be 動詞 ＋ 過去分詞≫という形で表します。これに対して、これまで学習してきた「～は…する」のように、何かに働きかける意味を表す文を**能動態**と言います。

　能動態にするか受動態にするかは、話題になっている「もの」や「こと」によって決まります。次の例文では、話題が「ショッピングモール」なので受動態が使われるわけです。

There is a shopping mall nearby. It's called Mountain Grove.

（近くにショッピングモールがあります。それはマウンテン・グローブという名前です）

この例文は "People call it Mountain Grove." のように能動態で表現することも可能ですが、受動態で表現する方が自然です。また、過去分詞は、start → started（過去形）→ started（過去分詞）のように、多くの場合動詞の過去形と同じ形ですが、begin → began（過去形）→ begun（過去分詞）のように不規則に変化するものもあります。巻末資料を参考にしながら下の表の空欄に適切な動詞の形を書き入れ確認しましょう。

不規則動詞の変化パターン	原形	過去形	過去分詞形
A-A-A （原形、過去形、過去分詞がすべて同じ）	cost put	cost	cost
A-B-A （原形と過去分詞が同じ）	become run		
A-B-B （過去形と過去分詞が同じ）	bring meet		
A-B-C （原形、過去形、過去分詞がすべて異なる）	speak write		

受動態にも能動態と同じように、過去形や未来表現、進行形などがあります。下の例文の日本語訳を完成させながら使い方を確認しましょう。

過去形は≪was / were ＋ 過去分詞≫となります。

I was given a placement test on the first day.

(　　　　　　　　　　　　　　　　　　　)

My class will be decided based on that result.

(　　　　　　　　　　　　　　　　　　　)

未来表現は≪will be ＋ 過去分詞≫や≪be going to be ＋ 過去分詞≫を使います。

 Let's Listen!　　　　　会話の大意を聞き取ろう！

タカシとドナの会話を聞いて、質問に対する答えとして最も適切なものを（A）〜（C）の中から１つ選びましょう。 1-33

Question 1　What does Takashi say about his new friends?

(A) They are from the same country.

(B) They are from the same university.

(C) They were in the same group during the tour.

Question 2　What does Takashi want to buy?

(A) Books and clothes

(B) Books and stationery

(C) Clothes and stationery

Question 3　What does Donna suggest?

(A) They should go to the shopping mall.

(B) Takashi should invite his friends to her house.

(C) They should eat dinner with Ron.

Let's Check & Read Aloud!

1. スクリプトを見ながら会話をもう1度聞き、下線部に当てはまる表現を書き入れましょう。（下線部には単語が2つ入ります）
2. 内容を確認して、全文を音読してみましょう。
3. タカシとドナの役割をパートナーと一緒に演じてみましょう。

 1-33

Let's Practice the Roleplay!

Donna's Role　　Takashi's Role

Donna speaks to Takashi in the living room.

Donna	How was your first day at school, Takashi?

Takashi Well, it was a busy day. I had a test, an orientation, and a ① _____ .
I ② _____ some new friends.

Donna That's good ③ _____ . Tell me about them.

Takashi OK. Ken is from Japan and Yoona is from South Korea. They are both college students. We were in the ④ _____ for the campus tour. After school we went to a shopping mall nearby, but it ⑤ _____ .

Donna That's too bad. Do you want to go shopping?

Takashi Yes, I want to buy ⑥ _____ and stationery. Is there a shopping mall around here?

Donna Yes, it's called Mountain Grove and is only a 10-minute drive from here. Well, Ron is ⑦ _____ today, so we could go to the mall now and have dinner there. How does ⑧ _____ ?

Takashi That would be great. Thank you so much.

〰〰 音読のヒント ✦

orientation や tour など、カタカナ英語として定着している単語は、「オリエンテーション」や「ツアー」のように読んでしまいがちですが、正しく「オリエンティション」[ɔ̀:riəntéiʃən]、「トゥア」[túər]と発音するようにしましょう。また、clothes も「クロウジィズ」と発音しがちですが、正しくは「クロウズ」[klóuz]です。気をつけましょう。

Grammar

文法に強くなろう！

A. 例にならい、枠の中から適切な単語を選び、必要な場合は適切な形にして次の１～４の文を完成させましょう。

例 English (*is spoken*) in many countries.

close
hold
speak ✓
steal
use

1. A welcome party for new students (   ) last night.

2. This shopping mall (   ) on Mondays, so let's try this weekend.

3. Instagram (   ) around the world.

4. My credit card (   ) while I was shopping.

B. 例にならい、カッコ内から正しい語句を選び○で囲みましょう。

例 The shopping mall (calls /（is called）) Mountain Grove.

1. The results of the placement test will (give / be given) next week.

2. The placement test (lasts / is lasted) for an hour.

3. Ron had a traffic accident and (took / was taken) to hospital.

4. This restaurant is known (by / for) its spicy foods.

C. 日本語の意味に合うようにカッコ内の語句を並べ替え、英文を完成させましょう。ただし、文の始めにくる単語も小文字にしてあり、１つ余分な語句が含まれています。

1. 今日、授業はありません。

   (no / be / holding / held / will / classes) today.

   _____

2. 先生が病気のため、今日の授業は休講になりました。

   (was / canceled / to / due / were / today's class) the teacher's illness.

   _____

3. そのショッピングモールは来月で閉鎖になります。

   (the / closed / close / be / will / shopping mall) next month.

   _____

4. このレストランはみんなに愛されています。

   (loving / restaurant / loved / this / by / is) everyone.

   _____

 **Let's Read!**

次のポスターを読み、その内容について１〜３の質問に答えましょう。 1-34

International Students! Feeling homesick?

Campus life away from home can be stressful. Sometimes you'll feel a little lost and miss your family and friends back home.

Don't <u>Drop Out</u>—Drop In!

Come and talk to us at the Drop-In Center about any problems you might be having: homesickness, loneliness, anything at all. We offer a free on-campus counseling service. You don't need an appointment. Just drop in, and we'll welcome you with coffee and cookies. Our experienced listeners will try to help you. You'll find us in the lobby of the Rennie Building, next to the Baker's Oven Café.

1. The underlined phrase "drop out" means _____.

   (A) break the rules

   (B) quit your studies

   (C) feel lonely and sad

2. Which sentence is true?

   (A) You need to make a reservation for the counseling service.

   (B) The Drop-In Center will welcome you if you bring coffee and cookies.

   (C) The Drop-In Center wants to help students who are having difficulties.

3. Where is the Drop-In Center?

   (A) Next to the Rennie Building

   (B) Beside the Baker's Oven Café

   (C) In the Baker's Oven Café

 [Notes]

appointment: 予約　　　experienced: 経験豊富な

Challenge Yourself!

Part I PHOTOGRAPHS

(A)～(C) の英文を聞き、写真の描写として最も適切なものを選びましょう。 1-35

1.

(A)　　　(B)　　　(C)

2.

(A)　　　(B)　　　(C)

Part II QUESTION-RESPONSE

最初に聞こえてくる英文に対する応答として最も適切なものを (A)～(C) の中から選びましょう。 1-36

3.　(A)　　　(B)　　　(C)

4.　(A)　　　(B)　　　(C)

Part III SHORT CONVERSATIONS

会話を聞き、下の英文が会話の内容と合っていれば T (True)、間違っていれば F (False) を○で囲みましょう。 1-37

5. The man talked with his parents yesterday.　　　　　　　T　　　F

6. The man isn't getting enough food from his homestay family.　　T　　　F

 Let's Read Aloud & Write!

授業のまとめとして、今日学習した対話文を 3 回書き写してしっかり覚えましょう。1 度英文を声に出して読んでから書き写すと頭に残りやすくなります。

今日のまとめ

英語で答えられますか？　　　Do you want to study abroad?

文法 助動詞

ホストファミリーが外出した夜、タカシは近くのレストランで外食をします。会話では、注文したり、希望を尋ねたりする際の表現を学びます。また、文法では**助動詞**に焦点を当てて学習します。

Warm-up

授業前に確認しておこう！

>> *Vocabulary Preview*

1 〜 10 の語句の意味として適切なものを a 〜 j の中から選びましょう。　🎵 1-38

1. bake   _____
2. care for   _____
3. main course _____
4. soup   _____
5. dessert   _____
6. meal   _____
7. medium   _____
8. order   _____
9. steak   _____
10. else   _____

a. 食事
b. ステーキ
c. 注文する
d. 主料理、メイン料理
e. 〜が欲しい
f. （肉の焼き具合が）中くらいの
g. （パンなどをオーブンで）焼く
h. デザート
i. スープ
j. その他の

ビートに乗って 1 〜 10 の語句を発音してみましょう。

>> *Grammar Point : 助動詞*

This restaurant <u>must</u> be very popular.

（このレストランはとても人気があるに違いありません）

<u>Could</u> I have some more coffee?

（コーヒーのお代わりをいただけますか？）

　助動詞は動詞の前につけて動詞に意味を追加するものです。助動詞の場合、一般動詞と違って主語が 3 人称単数であっても語尾に –s や –es がつくことはありません。
　主な助動詞とその用法は下の表の通りです。

can	〜できる（be able to） 〜してもよい	must	〜しなければならない（have to） 〜に違いない
may	〜してもよい 〜かもしれない	might	〜かもしれない
should	〜すべきである	used to	以前は〜だった

must の否定形 must not は「〜してはいけない」という意味になり、「〜する必要はない」と言いたい場合は don't have to を使います。また、would と could はそれぞれ助動詞 will と can の過去形ですが、実際のコミュニケーションにおいては過去の意味で使うのではなく、丁寧な言い方をする場合によく用いられます。

would like	〜をいただきたいのですが	※ want や want to よりも丁寧で控えめな感じがします。
would like to	〜したいのですが	
Would you ... ?	〜していただけないでしょうか？	※ Will you ... ？や Can you ... ？よりも丁寧で控えめな感じがします。
Could you ... ?		

上の表を参考にして、下の例文の日本語訳を完成させましょう。

疑問文にするときは助動詞を文の始めに置きます。

We'd like a table for two, please.
(   )

We're full right now. Would you like to wait?
(   )

How long is the wait?   (   )

It shouldn't be very long. Would you mind waiting for about 10 minutes?
(   )

否定文にするときは助動詞のすぐ後に not をつけます。

Let's Listen!

会話の大意を聞き取ろう！

タカシと接客係の会話を聞いて、質問に対する答えとして最も適切なものを (A)〜(C) の中から１つ選びましょう。

 1-39

Question 1　What does Takashi order for starters?

(A) Onion soup
(B) Chicken salad
(C) Potato soup

Question 2　What is the main dish that Takashi orders?

(A) Chicken wings
(B) Sirloin steak
(C) T-bone steak

Question 3　Does Takashi order any dessert?

(A) Yes, he orders some chocolate ice cream.
(B) Yes, he orders a cake.
(C) No, he just orders a cappuccino.

Let's Check & Read Aloud! 音読してみよう！

1. スクリプトを見ながら会話をもう1度聞き、下線部に当てはまる表現を書き入れ 1-39
   ましょう。（下線部には単語が2つ入ります）
2. 内容を確認して、全文を音読してみましょう。
3. タカシと接客係の役割をパートナーと一緒に演じてみましょう。

Let's Practice the Roleplay!

Server's Role   Takashi's Role

Takashi is ordering at a restaurant.

Server	Welcome to Taylor's Steak House. May I ①_____ something to start?
Takashi	Yes, I'll have the French onion soup, please.
Server	Certainly. What would you like ②_____ for your main course?
Takashi	I'd like the T-bone steak with a ③_____ .
Server	OK. How would you like your steak?
Takashi	Medium, please.
Server	Sure. Would you like something ④_____ ?
Takashi	Just water, please.
Server	Would you like ⑤_____ with your meal?
Takashi	No, that will ⑥_____ for now. Thanks.
Server	And would you ⑦_____ any dessert?
Takashi	Well, I'd like some chocolate cake and a cappuccino※, please.
Server	OK. Thanks. I'll be ⑧_____ .

[Note] ※cappuccino：カプチーノ（泡立てたミルクをのせたコーヒー）

ᗯᗯ 音読のヒント💡

"How would you like your steak?" は、肉の焼き加減の好みを聞く際の決まり文句です。会話に出てきた medium の他、well-done（十分焼けた）や rare（生焼けの、レアの）などがよく使われます。また、ティーボーンステーキはT字型の骨がついたステーキのことですが、他にはサーロインステーキ（sirloin steak）やリブステーキ（rib steak）などがあります。音読に慣れてきたら、肉の種類や焼き加減の他、飲み物やデザートを自分の好みの表現に入れ替えてみるとより実用的な練習になります。

Grammar

A. 例にならい、枠の中から適切な語句を選んで次の１〜４の文を完成させましょう。

例 (May) I take your order?

1. (　　　　　） you check on our order?

2. How long do we (　　　　） wait?

3. Let's eat out tonight, (　　　　） we?

4. There (　　　　） be a popular Italian restaurant here.

used to
could
may ✓
have to
shall

B. 例にならい、カッコ内から正しい語句を選び○で囲みましょう。

例　How (can /(would)) you like to pay?

1. "(Could I / Could you) have some more coffee?" "Sure. I'll be right back."

2. (I'd like / I'd like to) book a table for tonight, please.

3. (I'd like / I'd like to) my steak medium, please.

4. (Shall we / Shall you) have lunch together?

C. 日本語の意味に合うようにカッコ内の語句を並べ替え、英文を完成させましょう。ただし、文の始めにくる単語も小文字にしてあり、１つ余分な語句が含まれています。

1. あなたと同じものにします。

(you / as / have / I'm going / I'll / the same).

_____

2. お水をいただけますか？

(get / you / some / shall / could / me) water?

_____

3. お手洗いはどこでしょうか？

Where (wash / hands / I / can / am / my)?

_____

4. ご注文は何になさいますか？

What (you / have / I / would / like / to)?

_____

 **Let's Read!**

次のパッセージを読み、その内容について 1 ～ 3 の質問に答えましょう。 1-40

Tipping at a Restaurant

You enjoy a nice meal in a restaurant, then you have to pay the bill. But different countries have different customs. Should you leave a tip? And if so, how much? In the U.S., <u>servers</u> usually work for minimum wage, so they're happy to get tips. Minimum wage can vary, state by state, and in some states it's very low. If you don't tip, the server may get very little pay, ☐ most people choose to tip. The general rule is that the tip should be 15-20% of the cost of the meal. Of course, if the service is bad, you don't need to tip.

---

1. The underlined word "servers" means _____.

   (A) special tables in a restaurant

   (B) people who bring food to the table in a restaurant

   (C) people who pay the bill

2. The word that belongs in the ☐ in this passage is _____.

   (A) so

   (B) but

   (C) because

3. Which sentence is true?

   (A) American people always leave a tip for the server at a restaurant.

   (B) Minimum wage is the same all over the U.S.

   (C) The amount you tip is widely understood to be between 15 and 20%.

 [Notes]

bill: 勘定書　　wage: 賃金　　state: 州

Challenge Yourself!　　　　　　　　　　　リスニング力を試そう！

（A）〜（C）の英文を聞き、写真の描写として最も適切なものを選びましょう。 1-41

1.

　　　　（A）　　　（B）　　　（C）

2.

　　　　（A）　　　（B）　　　（C）

最初に聞こえてくる英文に対する応答として最も適切なものを（A）〜（C）の中 1-42
から選びましょう。

3.　（A）　　　（B）　　　（C）

4.　（A）　　　（B）　　　（C）

会話を聞き、下の英文が会話の内容と合っていれば T（True）、間違っていれば 1-43
F（False）を○で囲みましょう。

5. The woman was satisfied with the service in the restaurant.　　　T　　　F

6. The man doesn't want a well-cooked steak.　　　T　　　F

 Let's Read Aloud & Write!　　　　音読筆写で覚えよう！

授業のまとめとして、今日学習した対話文を3回書き写して
しっかり覚えましょう。1度英文を声に出して読んでから書き
写すと頭に残りやすくなります。

今日のまとめ

英語で答えられますか？　　　Do you often eat out?

UNIT 08 How long have you felt this way?

文法 現在完了形

体調を崩してしまったタカシは大学内にあるヘルスセンターを受診します。会話では、期間を尋ねたり、症状を述べたりする際の表現を学びます。また、文法では**現在完了形**に焦点を当てて学習します。

Warm-up　　　　　　　　　　　授業前に確認しておこう！

≫ Vocabulary Preview

1 ～ 10 の語句の意味として適切なものを a ～ j の中から選びましょう。　　CD 1-44

1. fever	＿＿＿	a.	薬
2. headache	＿＿＿	b.	息をする
3. sore	＿＿＿	c.	休む、くつろぐ
4. throat	＿＿＿	d.	ヒリヒリする、痛い
5. runny	＿＿＿	e.	のど
6. medicine	＿＿＿	f.	現在、今のところ
7. take off	＿＿＿	g.	熱
8. breathe	＿＿＿	h.	鼻水が出る
9. at the moment	＿＿＿	i.	～を脱ぐ
10. take it easy	＿＿＿	j.	頭痛

ビートに乗って 1 ～ 10 の語句を発音してみましょう。

≫ Grammar Point : 現在完了形

I've *already* <u>seen</u> a doctor, so I'll go to bed and get some rest today.

（もう医者には診てもらったので、今日はベッドに入って少し休息をとります）

> 否定文にするには have/has の後に not をつけます。
> また、会話では短縮形がよく使われます。

I <u>haven't seen</u> a doctor *yet*.　　　　　　（まだ医者には診てもらっていません）

<u>Have</u> you <u>had</u> this problem *before*?　　　（以前にもこういうことがありましたか？）

> 疑問文にするには have/has を主語の前に持ってきます。

　過去にしたことや過去に起こったことを現在と結びつけて話す場合には**現在完了形**を用い、≪ have/has ＋ 過去分詞≫という形で表します。主語が he など 3 人称単数の場合は have ではなく has を使います。現在完了形は、現在の状況を述べる言い方なので、last month など、明確に過去の時点を表す表現とは一緒に使いません。次の表で過去形との違いを確認しましょう。

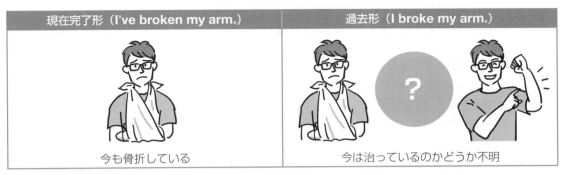

	現在完了形（**I've broken my arm.**）	過去形（**I broke my arm.**）
	今も骨折している	今は治っているのかどうか不明

また、現在完了形の表す意味にはいくつか種類があり、just（ちょうど今）や already（すでに）、yet（もうすでに、まだ）などの副詞が意味を見極める上でのポイントになります。次の表の例文の日本語訳を完成させながらそれぞれの意味を確認しましょう。

完了	～してしまった	"<u>Have</u> you <u>taken</u> your medicine *yet*?" "Yes. I took it this morning." ( )
	～したところだ	"<u>Have</u> you <u>taken</u> your medicine *yet*?" "Yes. I've *just* <u>taken</u> it." ( )
経験	～したことがある	<u>Have</u> you <u>been hospitalized</u> during the past two years? ( )
継続	ずっと～している	Ron <u>has been</u> in the hospital for two weeks. ( )

Let's Listen!　　　　会話の大意を聞き取ろう！

タカシと医師の会話を聞いて、質問に対する答えとして最も適切なものを（A）～（C）の中から１つ選びましょう。 1-45

Question 1　How long has Takashi been feeling sick?

(A) For a couple of days
(B) For a week
(C) For a few weeks

Question 2　What does the doctor ask Takashi?

(A) The name of the medicine he took
(B) Whether he is taking any medicine or not
(C) Where he bought his medicine

Question 3　What does the doctor tell Takashi to do?

(A) Drink a lot of water with meals
(B) Take the medicine once a day
(C) Take the medicine three times a day

Let's Check & Read Aloud!　　　　音読してみよう！

1. スクリプトを見ながら会話をもう１度聞き、下線部に当てはまる表現を書き入れ 1-45
   ましょう。（下線部には単語が２つ入ります）
2. 内容を確認して、全文を音読してみましょう。
3. タカシと医師の役割をパートナーと一緒に演じてみましょう。

Let's Practice the Roleplay!

Doctor's Role　　Takashi's Role

Takashi goes to see a doctor at the Health Center.

Doctor: Hello, Takashi. I'm Dr. Johnson. What ①＿＿＿＿＿＿＿＿＿＿ be the problem?

Takashi: Well, I have a fever and a headache. I also have a sore throat and a
②＿＿＿＿＿＿＿＿＿＿ .

Doctor: How long have you ③＿＿＿＿＿＿＿＿＿＿ way?

Takashi: It started a few days ago.

Doctor: I see. Could you ④＿＿＿＿＿＿＿＿＿＿ your shirt, please?

Takashi: Of course.

Doctor: Now ⑤＿＿＿＿＿＿＿＿＿＿ . Well, it doesn't sound good. Let me check your
throat. It looks red. I think ⑥＿＿＿＿＿＿＿＿＿＿ a cold.

Takashi: What should I do?

Doctor: Are you taking ⑦＿＿＿＿＿＿＿＿＿＿ at the moment?

Takashi: No, I'm not.

Doctor: Then, take this medicine three times a day after meals. You should also take
⑧＿＿＿＿＿＿＿＿＿＿ and rest at home for a few days.

Takashi: OK, I will. Thank you very much, Doctor.

〰〰 音読のヒント 💡

音の連結はすでに Unit 3 で取り上げましたが、こうした連結は必ずしも２語に限ったものではありません。３語でも４語でも、それが意味上１つの単位をなしている場合には音がつながって聞こえます。例えば、take it easy は「テイク・イット・イージー」ではなく、「テイキッリーズィ」のようにつながって聞こえます。音読する際はモデル音声を忠実にまねてみましょう。

 **Grammar**

A. 例にならい、枠の中から適切な単語を選び、必要な場合は適切な形にして次の 1 〜 4 の文を完成させましょう。

> 例 The hospital (*was*) crowded yesterday.

```
take
go
see
feel
be ✓
```

1. "What seems to be the problem?" "I'm not (   ) very well, Doctor."

2. I've already (   ) this medicine.

3. I (   ) to the dentist two days ago.

4. I think you should (   ) a doctor.

B. 例にならい、カッコ内から正しい語句を選び○で囲みましょう。

> 例 I've had a bad cold (since /(for)) a week.

1. Donna has had a high fever (since / for) yesterday.

2. The doctor (told / has told) me to take this medicine yesterday.

3. When (did the pain start / has the pain started)?

4. I haven't seen a doctor (already / yet).

C. 日本語の意味に合うようにカッコ内の語句を並べ替え、英文を完成させましょう。ただし、文の始めにくる単語も小文字にしてあり、1 つ余分な語句が含まれています。

1. 医者には見てもらいましたか？

(saw / doctor / have / a / you / seen)?

_____

2. いつから具合が悪いのですか？

(have / had / having / long / you / how) this problem?

_____

3. 歯医者からちょうど帰ってきたところです。

(back / come / came / the dentist / from / I've just).

_____

4. もうすでに 30 分もここで待っています。

(since / for / been / waiting / here / I've) 30 minutes already.

_____

次のパッセージを読み、その内容について 1 ～ 3 の質問に答えましょう。 1-46

Miles, Yards, Feet and Gallons

Japanese visitors to the U.S. will notice cultural differences as soon as they leave the airport. Distances on roads are measured in miles. Shorter distances are measured in yards and feet. On a hot summer day, you might be shocked to see the temperature outside the car may be over 95°, but don't worry. That's Fahrenheit, not Celsius! It's just 35°C. When drivers stop for gas, they fill up their cars in gallons, not liters. Families shopping at the supermarket may also buy a gallon of milk. The gallon is 3.785 liters in the U.S., so milk cartons are much larger than in Japan.

1. Japanese visitors arriving at a U.S. airport _____ wait long to feel they are in a different culture.

   (A) need to

   (B) must

   (C) won't have to

2. Car journeys in the U.S. are measured in _____.

   (A) kilometers

   (B) miles

   (C) feet and inches

3. Which sentence is true?

   (A) Fahrenheit is a unit of measurement of temperature in the U.S.

   (B) The Fahrenheit scale is familiar to most people living in Japan.

   (C) People in the U.S. used to measure milk in gallons, but they use liters now.

 [Notes]

measure: 測定する   mile: マイル（長さの単位で、1 マイルは約 1.6km）
yard: ヤード（長さの単位で、1 ヤードは 91.44cm）   foot: フィート（長さの単位で、
1 フィートは 30.48 cm）   Fahrenheit: 華氏（°F のように記す）
Celsius: 摂氏   °C: = degrees Celsius   gallon: ガロン（液量単位）

Challenge Yourself!

Part I PHOTOGRAPHS

(A)～(C) の英文を聞き、写真の描写として最も適切なものを選びましょう。 1-47

1.
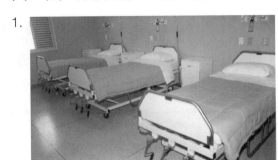
(A)　　(B)　　(C)

2.

(A)　　(B)　　(C)

Part II QUESTION-RESPONSE

最初に聞こえてくる英文に対する応答として最も適切なものを (A)～(C) の中から選びましょう。 1-48

3.　(A)　　(B)　　(C)

4.　(A)　　(B)　　(C)

Part III SHORT CONVERSATIONS

会話を聞き、下の英文が会話の内容と合っていれば T (True)、間違っていれば F (False) を○で囲みましょう。 1-49

5. The forecast looks wet for the rest of the week. 　　T　　F

6. The weather is likely to be hot for the rest of the week. 　　T　　F

Let's Read Aloud & Write!

授業のまとめとして、今日学習した対話文を３回書き写してしっかり覚えましょう。１度英文を声に出して読んでから書き写すと頭に残りやすくなります。

今日のまとめ

英語で答えられますか？　　What do you do to stay healthy?

UNIT 09 I think I'm lost.

文法 **形容詞・副詞**

ロサンゼルスを観光していたタカシは途中で道に迷ってしまい、通行人に道を尋ねます。会話では、援助を求めたり、道順を示したりする際の表現を学びます。また、文法では**形容詞・副詞**に焦点を当てて学習します。

Warm-up
授業前に確認しておこう！

>> **Vocabulary Preview**

1〜10の語句の意味として適切なものをa〜jの中から選びましょう。 🎵 1-50

1. past	_____	a.	真っすぐに
2. miss	_____	b.	劇場、映画館
3. museum	_____	c.	喜び
4. lost	_____	d.	道に迷った
5. huge	_____	e.	〜のそばを（通り）過ぎて
6. I'm afraid	_____	f.	博物館
7. pleasure	_____	g.	大通り
8. straight	_____	h.	巨大な
9. theater	_____	i.	〜を見逃す
10. boulevard	_____	j.	残念ながら

ビートに乗って1〜10の語句を発音してみましょう。

>> **Grammar Point : 形容詞・副詞**

It's a **tall** building. You can't miss it.

（それは高層ビルです。見過ごすことはありません）[形容詞]

I **almost** missed the bus.

（私はもう少しでバスに乗り遅れるところでした）[副詞]

　形容詞は、1番目の例文における tall のように、**名詞と結びついて人やものの状態や性質を説明するもの**です。形容詞は名詞の直前に置かれる他、"The building is tall." のように、動詞の後に置いて主語（＝名詞・代名詞）に説明を加えたりします。それに対し、**副詞**は、2番目の例文における almost のように、動詞や形容詞、他の副詞といった**名詞以外のものと結びついて様子や場所、時、頻度などを説明するもの**です。次の表で副詞の種類を確認しましょう。

「様態」（どのように）を表す	well, fast など	Could you speak more <u>slowly</u>?
「場所」（どこで）を表す	here, home など	I want to go <u>home</u> but I'm lost.
「時」（いつ）を表す	late, soon など	I got lost on the way and came home very <u>late</u> at night.
「頻度」（どれくらいの度合いで）を表す	always, often など	I can <u>never</u> read maps well. I'm bad with directions, so I <u>always</u> get lost.
「程度」（どれだけ）を表す	barely, hardly など	I'm sorry I can't help you. I <u>hardly</u> know the area.

一般動詞の前、be 動詞・助動詞の後に置くのが基本です。

修飾する語句の直前が基本。ただし動詞を修飾する場合は一般動詞の前、be 動詞・助動詞の後に置きます。

　一般に、副詞は usually や easily のように –ly で終わるものが多いですが、hard（懸命に、激しく）と hardly（ほとんど～でない）、late（遅れて）と lately（最近）のように、似た副詞で意味の異なるものがあります。また、形容詞に関しても、few と a few や little と a little など、a の有無で意味が異なりますので注意が必要です。

　下の例文の日本語訳を完成させながら使い方を確認しましょう。

a few は「（数について）少しはある」、few は「（数について）ほとんどない」となります。

You need to walk <u>a few</u> more blocks to get there. It'll take about five minutes.

（　　　　　　　　　　　　　　　　）

I have <u>little</u> sense of direction, so I often get lost.

（　　　　　　　　　　　　　　　　）

a little は「（量について）少しはある」、little は「（量について）ほとんどない」となります。

 Let's Listen!　　　会話の大意を聞き取ろう！

タカシと通行人の会話を聞いて、質問に対する答えとして最も適切なものを (A)～(C) の中から1つ選びましょう。 1-51

Question 1　Where does Takashi want to go?

(A) A museum
(B) A movie theater
(C) A movie studio

Question 2　What does Takashi ask the woman to do?

(A) Tell him how long it takes to get there
(B) Show him where he is on the map
(C) Take him to Hollywood Boulevard

Question 3　What should Takashi do on Hollywood Boulevard?

(A) He should go straight.
(B) He should turn right.
(C) He should turn left.

Let's Check & Read Aloud!

音読してみよう！

1. スクリプトを見ながら会話をもう 1 度聞き、下線部に当てはまる表現を書き入れましょう。（下線部には単語が 2 つ入ります）
2. 内容を確認して、全文を音読してみましょう。
3. タカシと通行人の役割をパートナーと一緒に演じてみましょう。

CD 1-51

Let's Practice the Roleplay!

Takashi's Role　Passerby's Role

Takashi speaks to a woman walking on the street.

Takashi Excuse me, ①________________ I'm lost. Can you help me?

Passerby Sure. Where would you like to go?

Takashi I'd like to go to the Hollywood Wax Museum. Could you show me ②________________ are on this map?

Passerby OK. We're here, at North McCadden Place.

Takashi Good. Then, I'm not very ③________________ the museum, right?

Passerby Yes, that's right. Go straight and ④________________ the movie theater. Then, turn left on Hollywood Boulevard. The museum will be ⑤________________ right.

Takashi After I turn left on Hollywood Boulevard, it would be on my right. Is that correct?

Passerby Yes. It's a huge building, so you ⑥________________ it.

Takashi Thank you so much. That's very ⑦________________ you.

Passerby My pleasure. I hope you'll find your ⑧________________ there.

Takashi Thanks. I'm sure I will.

音読のヒント

Hollywood Boulevard（ハリウッド大通り）の boulevard はしばしば街路名に用いられますが、発音が難しい単語です。「ブールバード」とカタカナ表記されることが多いですが、実際は「ブゥヴァードゥ」[búləvà:rd] のような感じですので気をつけて発音しましょう。また、North McCadden Place（ノースマカデン通り）の place もここでは「場所」という意味ではなく、街路名として使われています。

 **Grammar** 文法に強くなろう！

A. 例にならい、枠の中から適切な単語を選んで次の 1 ～ 4 の文を完成させましょう。

例　You speak English very (　well　).

1. How (　　　　　) will the next bus come?

2. I'm sorry. Could you speak more (　　　　　) ?

3. I'm a stranger here. I (　　　　　) know anything about this area.

4. "Why don't you take a taxi?" "No, it's (　　　　　) expensive."

> hardly
> slowly
> soon
> too
> well ✓

B. 例にならい、カッコ内から正しい語句を選び○で囲みましょう。

例　Be (careful / carefully) when you drive.

1. I'd like to go to Hollywood. Does this bus go (there / to there) ?

2. You're on the (wrong / wrongly) bus.

3. I'm (good / well) at reading maps.

4. I'm in a hurry. Could you go (little / a little) faster?

C. 日本語の意味に合うようにカッコ内の語句を並べ替え、英文を完成させましょう。ただし、文の始めにくる単語も小文字にしてあり、1 つ余分な語句が含まれています。

1. この近くに何か面白い観光名所はありますか？

(any / spots / tourist / there / are / interesting / interestingly) nearby?

_____

2. リトルトーキョーにはどのくらい時間がかかりますか？

(does / take / it / how / far / long) to Little Tokyo?

_____

3. 歩いて行くには遠すぎます。

(walk / to / it's / far / enough / too).

_____

4. （あなたは）間違った方向に向かっていますよ。

You're (in / direction / going / wrong / wrongly / the).

_____

Let's Read!

次のパッセージを読み、その内容について 1 〜 3 の質問に答えましょう。 1-52

Street, Road or Boulevard?

In English-speaking countries, you may find it difficult to understand the names of streets and public spaces. Here's a short guide to help you. A "lane" is usually a small, narrow road, often in a <u>rural area</u>. An "alley" is similar, but in an urban environment. A "street" refers to a road in a city, usually with buildings on one or both sides. An "avenue" or "boulevard" is a wide road in a city, often lined with trees. A "drive" is a type of street often found in a suburban area. Finally, a "place" is usually an area surrounded on four sides by buildings or streets.

1. The underlined phrase "rural area" means a place _____.

   (A) in the countryside

   (B) where two countries meet

   (C) with a lot of houses and buildings

2. _____ is usually a small, narrow road, often in an urban area.

   (A) A lane

   (B) A drive

   (C) An alley

3. Which sentence is true?

   (A) An avenue or boulevard is often blocked by trees.

   (B) There are often trees on both sides of an avenue or boulevard.

   (C) An avenue or boulevard is often found in a rural area.

 [Notes]

   urban: 都会の   environment: 環境
   suburban: 郊外の

Challenge Yourself!

Part I PHOTOGRAPHS

(A)〜(C) の英文を聞き、写真の描写として最も適切なものを選びましょう。 1-53

1.

(A)　　　(B)　　　(C)

2.

(A)　　　(B)　　　(C)

Part II QUESTION-RESPONSE

最初に聞こえてくる英文に対する応答として最も適切なものを (A)〜(C) の中から選びましょう。 1-54

3.　(A)　　　(B)　　　(C)

4.　(A)　　　(B)　　　(C)

Part III SHORT CONVERSATIONS

会話を聞き、下の英文が会話の内容と合っていれば T（True）、間違っていれば F（False）を○で囲みましょう。 1-55

5. The woman doesn't understand the man's explanation. 　　T　　　F

6. The man doesn't know the distance in kilometers. 　　T　　　F

 Let's Read Aloud & Write! 音読筆写で覚えよう！

授業のまとめとして、今日学習した対話文を３回書き写してしっかり覚えましょう。１度英文を声に出して読んでから書き写すと頭に残りやすくなります。

今日のまとめ

英語で答えられますか？　　Are you good at reading maps?

UNIT 10 Do you want me to take your picture?

文法 **不定詞**

ハリウッドを観光中のタカシは、1人で写真を
撮っている観光客に声をかけます。会話では、援
助を申し出たり、確認を求めたりする際の表現を
学びます。また、文法では**不定詞**に焦点を当てて
学習します。

 Warm-up　　　　　　　　　　　　授業前に確認しておこう！

≫ *Vocabulary Preview*

1 ～ 10 の語句の意味として適切なものを a ～ j の中から選びましょう。　　🎵 1-56

1. in front of	_____	a. 背景
2. gate	_____	b. 写真
3. background	_____	c. 主な、主要な
4. favor	_____	d. いくつかの、数枚の
5. press	_____	e. ボタン
6. main	_____	f. ～の前に
7. perfect	_____	g. ～を押す
8. button	_____	h. 門、入り口
9. photo	_____	i. 完璧な、申し分のない
10. several	_____	j. 親切な行為

ビートに乗って 1 ～ 10 の語句を発音してみましょう。

≫ *Grammar Point : 不定詞*

Is it OK <u>to take</u> pictures here?　　　　　　　　（ここで写真を撮ってもいいですか？）
I'm sorry <u>to bother</u> you, but could I ask you a favor?
　　　　　　　　　　（お邪魔してすみませんが、お願いをしてもよろしいですか？）
I have a lot of photos <u>to post</u> on Instagram.
　　　　　　　　　　（インスタグラムに投稿すべき写真がたくさんあります）

≪ to ＋動詞の原形≫の形を **to 不定詞**または単に**不定詞**と呼びますが、その用法は下の表のよう
に大きく 3 つに分けられます。

名詞的用法	～すること	I want <u>to post</u> this photo on Instagram.
副詞的用法	～するために（目的）	I got up very early this morning <u>to see</u> the sunrise.
	～して（感情の原因）	We're very happy <u>to see</u> you again.
形容詞的用法	～すべき	I have a favor <u>to ask</u> you.

> 形容詞的用法は名詞のすぐ後ろにきてその名詞を説明します。
> 「頼むべきお願いを持っている」→「お願いがある」

62

また、下の表のように、to 不定詞の前に what や how などの疑問詞がついてまとまった意味を表す他、≪形容詞／副詞 + enough + to 不定詞≫といった慣用表現もあります。例文の日本語訳を完成させながら使い方を確認しましょう。

疑問詞 + **to** 不定詞	Let me show you <u>how to use</u> this camera. ( )
動詞 + 人 + **to** 不定詞	What do you <u>want me to do</u>? ( )
enough や **too** を伴う 形容詞／副詞 + **to** 不定詞	The actor was <u>kind **enough** to take</u> a photo with me. ( ) I was <u>**too** excited to say</u> anything. ( )

≪ how + to 不定詞≫で「どのように〜したらよいのか、〜の仕方」となります。

≪ want + 人 + to 不定詞≫で「〜に…してほしい」となります。

≪形容詞／副詞 + enough + to 不定詞≫で「〜するには十分なくらい…だ」となります。

≪ too + 形容詞／副詞 + to 不定詞≫で「〜するにはあまりにも…過ぎる」となります。

 Let's Listen!   会話の大意を聞き取ろう！

タカシと観光客の会話を聞いて、質問に対する答えとして最も適切なものを (A)〜(C) の中から1つ選びましょう。 1-57

Question 1   What does Takashi ask the woman to do?

  (A) Take a photo with him

  (B) Take a photo of him

  (C) Look at the camera

Question 2   What does Takashi offer to do?

  (A) Take a photo of the woman

  (B) Draw a picture of the woman

  (C) Give his camera to the woman

Question 3   How many photos does the woman want?

  (A) Just one

  (B) Two

  (C) Several

Let's Check & Read Aloud! 音読してみよう！

1. スクリプトを見ながら会話をもう1度聞き、下線部に当てはまる表現を書き入れ 1-57
   ましょう。（下線部には単語が2つ入ります）
2. 内容を確認して、全文を音読してみましょう。
3. タカシと観光客の役割をパートナーと一緒に演じてみましょう。

Let's Practice the Roleplay!

Takashi's Role　Tourist's Role

*Takashi is talking to a tourist in front of
the TCL Chinese Theater.*

Takashi	Excuse me, could I ①_____ a favor? Could you take my photo, please?
Tourist	Sure. No problem.
Takashi	Thank you. Here you are. Press ②_____ , please.
Tourist	OK. Do you want the ③_____ in the background?
Takashi	Yes, please.
Tourist	Look at the camera and smile. There you go.
Takashi	Could you take one more, please?
Tourist	All right. Here. Please take a ④_____ this. Is it OK?
Takashi	Yes, ⑤_____ . Thank you so much. Well, would you like ⑥_____ take your picture?
Tourist	Oh, thank you. That ⑦_____ great.
Takashi	You're welcome. Do you need only one, or should I take ⑧_____ ?
Tourist	Could you take two, please?

〰〰 音読のヒント -ϙ̣-

単語の最後にくる l [l] の発音はすでに Unit 4 で取り上げましたが、単語の真ん中にくる l [l] もやはり「ル」ではなく「ゥ」のように聞こえます。例えば、welcome [wélkəm] は「ウェルカム」ではなく、むしろ「ウェゥカム」のように聞こえます。"You're welcome." はよく使う表現ですから、自信を持って発音できるよう音読練習をしましょう。

 **Grammar** 文法に強くなろう！

A. 例にならい、カッコ内に to が必要であれば to を、不要であれば×を書き入れましょう。

例 I want (to) take a lot of photos.

1. Let me (　　　　　) show you some pictures.

2. I'd like (　　　　　) ask you a favor.

3. I'd like (　　　　　) a table for two, please.

4. I have a favor (　　　　　) ask you.

B. 例にならい、枠の中から適切な単語を選び、to 不定詞の形にして次の 1 ～ 4 の文を完成させましょう。

例 Can you tell me where (to call)?

1. Are we allowed (　　　　　) pictures in this museum?

2. I hope (　　　　　) from you soon.

3. I'd like (　　　　　) up for a guided tour.

4. Take your time. There's no need (　　　　　).

call ✓
hear
hurry
sign
take

C. 日本語の意味に合うようにカッコ内の語句を並べ替え、英文を完成させましょう。ただし、文の始めにくる単語も小文字にしてあり、1 つ余分な語句が含まれています。

1. あの人に写真を頼みましょう。

Let's (that / man / take / ask / our picture / to take).

_____

2. お邪魔してすみませんが、写真を 1 枚撮っていただけませんか？

(to / I'm / you / sorry / bothering / bother), but could you take a picture for us?

_____

3. 他に何か頼みたいことはありませんか？

(do / me / you / want / want to / to) do anything else?

_____

4. 実は、それの使い方が全然わからないのです。

In fact, I don't know (it / how / what / to / use / at all).

_____

Let's Read!

読解力を高めよう！

次のパッセージを読み、その内容について 1 ～ 3 の質問に答えましょう。

 1-58

Taxi!

Japan has some of the finest taxi services in the world. Drivers are polite and wear uniforms and gloves. The passenger door opens and closes automatically, and there's no need to tip the driver. But don't expect these things overseas! In many countries a tip of around 10% is expected, although you can just say "Keep the change." If you see a taxi in the street, don't shout "Taxi!" This only works in movies! Just raise your hand, and try to catch their attention. Actually, it may not be easy to stop a taxi in the street. In most cases you'll need to phone or order one online.

1. In Japanese taxis, the passenger _____.

   (A) doesn't need to shut the door

   (B) has to leave a small tip

   (C) should wear gloves

2. In many cultures it's the custom for the driver to _____.

   (A) charge an extra 10% for the ride

   (B) tip the passenger

   (C) receive a tip from the passenger

3. Which sentence is true?

   (A) Shouting "Taxi!" is the best way to catch a taxi in the street.

   (B) If you want to take a taxi, you should call or order one online.

   (C) It's easy to stop a taxi in the street, so you don't have to call.

[Notes]

polite: 礼儀正しい   attention: 注意

Challenge Yourself!

Part I PHOTOGRAPHS

(A)〜(C) の英文を聞き、写真の描写として最も適切なものを選びましょう。 1-59

1.

(A)　　　(B)　　　(C)

2.

(A)　　　(B)　　　(C)

Part II QUESTION-RESPONSE

最初に聞こえてくる英文に対する応答として最も適切なものを (A)〜(C) の中から選びましょう。 1-60

3.　(A)　　　(B)　　　(C)

4.　(A)　　　(B)　　　(C)

Part III SHORT CONVERSATIONS

会話を聞き、下の英文が会話の内容と合っていれば T（True）、間違っていれば F（False）を○で囲みましょう。 1-61

5. The woman gives the taxi driver 20 dollars.　　　　　T　　　F

6. The driver tells the woman to go to Brooklyn.　　　　T　　　F

Let's Read Aloud & Write!

授業のまとめとして、今日学習した対話文を３回書き写してしっかり覚えましょう。１度英文を声に出して読んでから書き写すと頭に残りやすくなります。

> 今日のまとめ

英語で答えられますか？　　Do you post a lot of photos on social media?

UNIT 11   I've lost my phone.

 文法   分詞

博物館を訪ねた後、タカシは忘れ物に気づき、あわてて遺失物取扱所に向かいます。会話では、問題を述べたり、確信を示したりする際の表現を学びます。また、文法では**分詞**に焦点を当てて学習します。

Warm-up   授業前に確認しておこう！

≫ *Vocabulary Preview*

1 〜 10 の語句の意味として適切なものを a 〜 j の中から選びましょう。   🎵 1-62

1. realize   _____
2. gone   _____
3. lose   _____
4. text   _____
5. fill out   _____
6. entrance   _____
7. restroom   _____
8. right away   _____
9. hand in   _____
10. meantime   _____

a. すぐに
b. その間
c. （公共施設の）トイレ
d. （拾得物など）を届け出る、提出する
e. 〜だと気づく
f. （人・物が）いなくなった、なくなった
g. （携帯電話の）メール
h. （書式・用紙など）に記入する
i. 〜をなくす
j. 玄関、入り口

ビートに乗って 1 〜 10 の語句を発音してみましょう。

≫ *Grammar Point : 分詞*

Who is <u>the woman</u> **talking with the security officer over there**?

（あそこで警備員と話している女性は誰ですか？）［現在分詞］

My <u>lost</u> <u>wallet</u> was returned to me by the police.

（なくした財布が警察によって私に返却されました）［過去分詞］

分詞には**現在分詞**と**過去分詞**があり、これらは形容詞として使うことができます。上の例文のように、**現在分詞は「〜している」という能動的な意味、過去分詞は「〜された」という受動的な意味になります。**

形容詞には分詞から派生しているものがあり、感情を表す動詞から派生しているものは使い分けに注意が必要です。例えば、exciting と excited はもともと動詞 excite（「（人を）興奮させる」）のそれぞれ現在分詞、過去分詞なので、exciting は「（人を）興奮させるような」という能動の意味、excited は「興奮させられた（⇒興奮した）」という受動の意味を持ちます。次の表でそうした形容詞の使い方を確認しましょう。

-ing （物や事がどのようなものかを説明する）			-ed （人がどのように感じたかを説明する）		
This museum is	boring.	（退屈な）	I'm	bored.	（退屈している）
	exciting.	（刺激的な）		excited.	（興奮している）
	interesting.	（面白い）		interested.	（興味を持っている）

例文の日本語訳を完成させながら使い方分詞の用法を確認しましょう。

We keep <u>lost</u> property for three weeks.

(   )

1 語の場合は名詞の前に置きます。

I've lost my key. Are there any keys <u>kept as</u> <u>lost property here</u>?

(   )

他の語句が加わると名詞の後に置きます。

「have ＋ 目的語 ＋ 過去分詞」で「〈…を〉〈…して〉もらう、〈…〉される」となります。

<u>I had my bike</u> <u>stolen</u> just outside my house.

(   )

<u>I left my bike</u> <u>unlocked</u> yesterday and it was stolen.

(   )

「leave/keep ＋目的語＋補語」で「〈…を〉 ずっと〈…の状態に〉しておく」となります。

 ## Let's Listen!

会話の大意を聞き取ろう！

タカシと係員の会話を聞いて、質問に対する答えとして最も適切なものを（A）〜（C）の中から１つ選びましょう。

 1-63

Question 1　What did Takashi lose?

(A) His wallet

(B) His tablet computer

(C) His phone

Question 2　Where does Takashi say he lost it?

(A) At the entrance hall

(B) In the restroom on the first floor

(C) In the restroom on the second floor

Question 3　What will Takashi do next?

(A) Fill out a form

(B) Go to the restroom

(C) Call his friend

Let's Check & Read Aloud!

音読してみよう！

1. スクリプトを見ながら会話をもう1度聞き、下線部に当てはまる表現を書き入れ 1-63
   ましょう。（下線部には単語が2つ入ります）
2. 内容を確認して、全文を音読してみましょう。
3. タカシと係員の役割をパートナーと一緒に演じてみましょう。

Let's Practice the Roleplay!

Takashi's Role　　Clerk's Role

Takashi is talking to a clerk at the Lost and Found office.

Takashi　Excuse me. Has anyone ①＿＿＿＿＿＿＿＿＿ a phone? I think I've lost mine.

Clerk　I'm afraid we don't have any phones here right now. Do you know where ②＿＿＿＿＿＿＿＿＿ it?

Takashi　I'm ③＿＿＿＿＿＿＿＿＿ . I was on the tour and when it finished, I realized that the phone was gone.

Clerk　When did you ④＿＿＿＿＿＿＿＿＿ it?

Takashi　I sent a text to my friend from the entrance hall before the ⑤＿＿＿＿＿＿＿＿＿ .

Clerk　Did you use your phone during the tour?

Takashi　No, I don't think so. Wait. I think I ⑥＿＿＿＿＿＿＿＿＿ in the restroom on the first floor. I'm quite positive.

Clerk　OK. I'll ⑦＿＿＿＿＿＿＿＿＿ to check right away. In the meantime, could you ⑧＿＿＿＿＿＿＿＿＿ this lost and found form?

Takashi　Sure. Thanks for your help.

♪♪♪ 音読のヒント 💡

"I realized that the phone was gone." で使われている接続詞の that は、「～だと気づきました」の「と」に当たる表現ですから、読む際には弱く「ザット」[ðət] と発音します。また、ポーズを取るときはその前で取ります。例えば、"I think that it's too expensive." という文を読む際にどこかで息つぎをするとすれば、I think と that の間となります。実際には I think that の後で切ることもありますが、その場合は次に何を言おうか言葉に詰まって考えているときです。

Grammar

A. 例にならい、枠の中から適切な単語を選び、現在分詞か過去分詞にして次の 1 ～ 4 の文を完成させましょう。

例 The photos (*taken*) by Yoona are all gone!

1. The (　　　　　） bicycle was found near the museum.

2. I'm (　　　　　） for my suitcase. Could you help me?

3. I'm sorry to keep you (　　　　　）.

4. I had trouble (　　　　　） the Lost and Found office.

find
look
steal
take ✓
wait

B. 例にならい、カッコ内から正しい語句を選び○で囲みましょう。

例 Los Angeles is an ((exciting) / excited) city.

1. This museum is very (interesting / interested).

2. I was (shocking / shocked) to find that my passport was gone.

3. We have only two days (leaving / left) before returning to Japan.

4. I left my keys inside, and the door is (locking / locked).

C. 日本語の意味に合うようにカッコ内の語句を並べ替え、英文を完成させましょう。ただし、文の始めにくる単語も小文字にしてあり、1 つ余分な語句が含まれています。

1. 私の盗まれた電話はまだ見つかっていません。

(phone / hasn't / steal / stolen / been / my) found yet.

_____

2. ここに置いてあったスーツケースがなくなりました。

The suitcase (left / is / going / gone / here / I).

_____

3. いつそれがなくなっているのに気づきましたか？

When did (you / missed / missing / notice / was / it)?

_____

4. 空港でパスポートを盗まれました。

I had (stolen / stealing / passport / the / at / my) airport.

_____

 **Let's Read!**

次のポスターを読み、その内容について 1 ～ 3 の質問に答えましょう。 1-64

Stay Alert! Stay Safe!

One of the worst things that can happen on an overseas trip is to lose your wallet, passport or phone. How can you keep your valuables safe? A few simple rules will help. First, if you have valuables in your handbag, wear it over your shoulder and across your chest, not just on your shoulder. A bag with a zipper is a good choice. Second, never carry your wallet or phone in your back pocket. If you do, you're really asking for it to be stolen. And finally, be careful in crowded places, especially places that are popular with tourists.

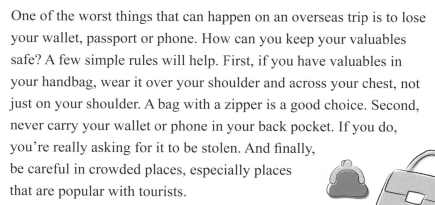

1. You should wear your bag over your shoulder and across your chest because it's
   _____.

   (A) easier to carry

   (B) easier to be stolen

   (C) more difficult to steal

2. It's _____ to carry your phone in your back pocket.

   (A) not a good idea

   (B) a great idea

   (C) advisable

3. Which sentence is true?

   (A) Thieves often target tourists in crowded places.

   (B) Tourists should avoid using a bag with a zipper.

   (C) Tourists don't have to be careful in crowded places.

 [Notes]

alert: 警戒して　　valuables: 貴重品　　chest: 胸

Challenge Yourself! リスニング力を試そう！

Part I PHOTOGRAPHS

(A)～(C) の英文を聞き、写真の描写として最も適切なものを選びましょう。 1-65

1.

(A)　　(B)　　(C)

2.

(A)　　(B)　　(C)

Part II QUESTION-RESPONSE

最初に聞こえてくる英文に対する応答として最も適切なものを (A)～(C) の中から選びましょう。 1-66

3.　(A)　　(B)　　(C)

4.　(A)　　(B)　　(C)

Part III SHORT CONVERSATIONS

会話を聞き、下の英文が会話の内容と合っていれば T（True）、間違っていれば F（False）を○で囲みましょう。 1-67

5. The woman will use a bag with a zipper.　　　　T　　　F

6. The man decides to follow the woman's advice.　　T　　　F

 Let's Read Aloud & Write! 　　音読筆写で覚えよう！

授業のまとめとして、今日学習した対話文を3回書き写してしっかり覚えましょう。1度英文を声に出して読んでから書き写すと頭に残りやすくなります。

今日のまとめ

英語で答えられますか？　　　Have you ever lost your phone or wallet?

UNIT 12 I love roller coasters!

文法 比較

タカシとユナは休日にアミューズメントパークへ出かけます。会話では、賛同したり、感想を述べたりする際の表現を学びます。また、文法では比較に焦点を当てて学習します。

Warm-up

授業前に確認しておこう！

» Vocabulary Preview

1 〜 10 の語句の意味として適切なものを a 〜 j の中から選びましょう。　🎵 1-68

1. mind	_____	a.	絶対に、もちろん
2. attraction	_____	b.	〜に乗る、（遊園地の）乗り物
3. scary	_____	c.	観覧車
4. scared	_____	d.	呼び物、人を引き付けるもの
5. dizzy	_____	e.	（物事が）恐ろしい
6. definitely	_____	f.	怖がって
7. height	_____	g.	高いところ
8. roller coaster	_____	h.	〜を嫌だと思う
9. Ferris wheel	_____	i.	ジェットコースター
10. ride	_____	j.	目が回って

ビートに乗って 1 〜 10 の語句を発音してみましょう。

» Grammar Point : 比較

This ride is <u>as scary as</u> the roller coaster.

（この乗り物はジェットコースターと同じくらい怖いです）

The Ferris wheel is much <u>more fun than</u> I thought.

（観覧車は思っていたよりもずっと面白いです）

This is one of <u>the most popular</u> sightseeing spots in Los Angeles.

（ここはロサンゼルスで最も人気がある観光地の 1 つです）

形容詞や副詞を使って「〜と同じくらい…だ」と 2 つのものを比較する場合、≪ as ＋ 形容詞／副詞 ＋ as ... ≫という形で表します。

また、「〜より面白い」や「最も面白い」のように、

	1 音節	2 音節	3 音節
比較級	-er		more 〜
最上級	-est		most 〜

他と比較しながら話す場合、「面白い」という形容詞の**比較級**や**最上級**を使って表現します。比較級や最上級にするには、**「1 音節の短い単語は語尾に -er（比較級）、-est（最上級）をつけ、3 音節以上の長い単語は前に more（比較級）、most（最上級）をつける」**が基本ですが、2 音節の単語は

両方のパターンがあります。また、不規則に変化するものも多くあります。
下の表を完成させながら確認しましょう。

> 音節については巻末資料を参照してください。

	原級	比較級	最上級	
1音節	high	higher	highest	語尾に -er / -est をつける（基本パターン）
	large	larger	largest	語尾に -r / -st をつける（-e で終わる単語）
	big			子音字を重ねて -er / -est をつける （<1母音字 ＋ 1子音字> で終わる単語）
2音節	early	earlier	earliest	y を i に変え -er / -est をつける （< 子音字 ＋ y > で終わる単語）
	simple	simpler	simplest	語尾に -(e)r / -(e)st をつける （-er, -le, -ow で終わる単語）
	slowly ※	more slowly	most slowly	前に more / most をつける （※形容詞に -ly がついた副詞は前に more / most をつける）
3音節以上	difficult	more difficult	most difficult	
	many / much	more	most	不規則な変化をする（例外的な単語）
	good / well			
	little			
	bad / badly / ill			

下の例文の日本語訳を完成させながら使い方を確認しましょう。

Come on! This roller coaster is<u>n't as scary as</u> you think.

(　　　　　　　　　　　　　　　　　　　　　　　　　　　)

This is the <u>most exciting</u> amusement park that I've ever visited.

(　　　　　　　　　　　　　　　　　　　　　　　　　　　)

 Let's Listen!　　　　　　会話の大意を聞き取ろう！

タカシとユナの会話を聞いて、質問に対する答えとして最も適切なものを（A）～（C）
の中から1つ選びましょう。 1-69

Question 1　How long will they have to wait to ride the roller coaster?

(A) Half an hour
(B) An hour
(C) An hour and a half

Question 2　What does Takashi say about waiting for the ride?

(A) He doesn't like waiting.
(B) He enjoys waiting.
(C) He doesn't mind waiting.

Question 3　What will they ride after this conversation?

(A) The tea-cup ride
(B) The Ferris wheel
(C) The roller coaster

Ferris wheel

Let's Check & Read Aloud!　　　　音読してみよう！

1. スクリプトを見ながら会話をもう1度聞き、下線部に当てはまる表現を書き入れましょう。（下線部には単語が2つ入ります）　 1-69
2. 内容を確認して、全文を音読してみましょう。
3. タカシとユナの役割をパートナーと一緒に演じてみましょう。

Let's Practice the Roleplay!

Takashi's Role　　Yoona's Role

Takashi and Yoona are at an amusement park.

(Takashi) What do you want to ①_____ ?

(Yoona) How about the roller coaster? I love roller coasters!

(Takashi) ②_____ ? That's the most popular attraction here.

(Yoona) Wow! Look at that line! They say the wait will be about ③_____ .

(Takashi) I don't ④_____ , but this roller coaster looks really scary. I'm a little scared.

After a while

(Yoona) It was a ⑤_____ fun!

(Takashi) Yes, but it was scary! I'm ⑥_____ . I want to go on something ⑦_____ so scary.

(Yoona) OK. Which do you like better, the Ferris wheel or the tea-cup ride? They are not scary.

(Takashi) Definitely the tea-cup ride. I'm afraid ⑧_____ .

(Yoona) That's fine. Let's go and stand in the line.

〰〰音読のヒント✿

音読する際には強弱に注意することが大切ですが、強勢を入れて発音することで様々な意味を伝えることができます。例えば対話の中の "Yes, but it was scary!" という英文では、was に強勢を置いて "Yes, but it WAS scary!" のように発音することで、「そうだね。だけど、（怖そうに見えるだけでなく）実際に怖かったよ」という意味を伝えることができます。

 **Grammar**　　　　　　　　　　　　　　　　　　　　文法に強くなろう！

A. 例にならい、空所に下線部の単語の比較級か最上級を入れて次の1～4の文を完成させましょう。

例　I can't run very <u>fast</u>. You run (*faster*) than me.

1. This amusement park is very <u>big</u>. It's (　　　　　　) than the one in my town.

2. The haunted house was very <u>scary</u>. It was (　　　　　　) than I expected.

3. This roller coaster is very <u>exciting</u>. It's the (　　　　　　) ride I've ever experienced.

4. This park is very <u>famous</u>. In fact, it's the (　　　　　　) tourist attraction here.

B. 例にならい、カッコ内から正しい語句を選び○で囲みましょう。

例　Yoona is the same age ((as) / than) Takashi.

1. There is a height limit. You have to be (taller / more tall) than 130 centimeters.

2. This new amusement park is (two / twice) as large as the old one.

3. This ride is (very / much) more fun than I thought.

4. The Ferris wheel is the most popular (in / of) all the rides here.

C. 日本語の意味に合うようにカッコ内の語句を並べ替え、英文を完成させましょう。ただし、文の始めにくる単語も小文字にしてあり、<u>1つ余分な語句が含まれています</u>。

1. ジェットコースターは思ったほど怖くありませんでした。

(as / scary / more / roller coaster / the / wasn't) as I thought.

＿＿＿＿＿＿＿＿＿＿＿＿＿＿＿＿＿＿＿＿＿＿＿＿＿＿＿＿＿＿＿＿

2. ジェットコースターはティーカップよりはるかに人気があります。

The roller coaster (more / than / popular / is / better / much) the tea-cup ride.

＿＿＿＿＿＿＿＿＿＿＿＿＿＿＿＿＿＿＿＿＿＿＿＿＿＿＿＿＿＿＿＿

3. 今1番人気のある乗り物は何ですか？

(is / popular / best / what / the / most) ride now?

＿＿＿＿＿＿＿＿＿＿＿＿＿＿＿＿＿＿＿＿＿＿＿＿＿＿＿＿＿＿＿＿

4. 1番好きなアミューズメントパークはどこですか？

Which (best / amusement park / you / like / better / do)?

＿＿＿＿＿＿＿＿＿＿＿＿＿＿＿＿＿＿＿＿＿＿＿＿＿＿＿＿＿＿＿＿

 **Let's Read!**

次のパッセージを読み、その内容について 1 〜 3 の質問に答えましょう。 1-70

Gifts

It's always nice to take a small gift for your homestay family, but it can be difficult to decide what gift to take. How old are the host family members? What are their interests? Japanese snacks may be a good choice, but remember, not everyone likes seaweed or little dried fish! A good gift is one that has some kind of cultural interest. If, for example, you give a nice set of chopsticks, you can explain how to use them. If you give a *daruma* doll, you can show your host family how to make a wish come true. They might wish to visit Japan sometime!

1. Before you decide what gift to take for your host family, you should _____.

    (A) think about your own age

    (B) consider their age and interests

    (C) ask them what they want

2. Seaweed is popular in Japan, _____.

    (A) so your host family will be happy to try it

    (B) but people in other countries prefer little dried fish

    (C) but people in other countries may not enjoy it

3. A *daruma* doll is mentioned as _____.

    (A) a gift of cultural interest

    (B) a dream come true

    (C) a very expensive gift

 [Notes]

seaweed: 海藻   chopsticks: 箸   come true: 実現する

Challenge Yourself! リスニング力を試そう！

Part I PHOTOGRAPHS

(A)～(C) の英文を聞き、写真の描写として最も適切なものを選びましょう。 1-71

1.

2.

    (A)   (B)   (C)   (A)   (B)   (C)

Part II QUESTION-RESPONSE

最初に聞こえてくる英文に対する応答として最も適切なものを (A)～(C) の中 1-72
から選びましょう。

3. (A)　　(B)　　(C)

4. (A)　　(B)　　(C)

Part III SHORT CONVERSATIONS

会話を聞き、下の英文が会話の内容と合っていれば T（True）、間違っていれば 1-73
F（False）を○で囲みましょう。

5. At first, the man didn't know what a *shamoji* is used for.　　　　T　　　F

6. The woman asks where to buy a T-shirt for her father.　　　　T　　　F

 Let's Read Aloud & Write! 音読筆写で覚えよう！

授業のまとめとして、今日学習した対話文を 3 回書き写して
しっかり覚えましょう。1 度英文を声に出して読んでから書き
写すと頭に残りやすくなります。

今日のまとめ

英語で答えられますか？　　　What's your favorite ride at an amusement park?

UNIT 13 Let me introduce my friend.

文法 関係詞

タカシはレーガン家のホームパーティに友人のユナを招待します。会話では、人を紹介したり、手みやげを渡したりする際の表現を学びます。また、文法では関係詞に焦点を当てて学習します。

Warm-up

授業前に確認しておこう！

≫ Vocabulary Preview

1 ～ 10 の語句の意味として適切なものを a ～ j の中から選びましょう。

🎵 1-74

1. introduce	_____	a.	～のことになると
2. barbecue	_____	b.	庭
3. yard	_____	c.	専門家
4. invite	_____	d.	くつろいで、気楽に
5. at home	_____	e.	～を紹介する
6. have a seat	_____	f.	夫
7. when it comes to	_____	g.	バーベキュー
8. expert	_____	h.	～を当てにする
9. count on	_____	i.	～を招待する
10. husband	_____	j.	座る

ビートに乗って 1 ～ 10 の語句を発音してみましょう。

≫ Grammar Point : 関係詞

We need someone who can teach us how to dance.

（私たちにはダンスの方法を教えてくれる人が必要です）

I have a friend whose father is a popular actor.

（私には父親が人気俳優である友人がいます）

We enjoyed eating the Korean dessert that Yoona made.

（私たちはユナが作った韓国のデザートを美味しくいただきました）

「ダンスの方法を教えてくれる人」のように、下線部分と名詞（この場合は「人」をつなぐ（関係づける）働きをするのが**関係代名詞**です。関係代名詞で説明される名詞を**先行詞**と呼びますが、その先行詞が人かそうでないかによって関係代名詞は次の表のような使い分けをします。

先行詞	主格	所有格	目的格
人	who	whose	who / whom
人以外	which	whose	which
人・人以外	that	—	that

> 目的格の関係代名詞はよく省略されます。また、口語では that 以外はあまり使われません。

1番目の例文は次の2つの文を1つにしたものと考えればよいでしょう。

A. We need <u>someone</u>.
B. <u>He</u> can teach us how to dance.

➡ We need someone <u>who</u> can teach us how to dance.

下線部分の someone と he は同一人物なのでここを関係代名詞でつなぐわけですが、he は元の文の主語なので主格の関係代名詞 who を使います。同様に、3番目の例文は次の2文を1つにしたものです。下線部分の a Korean dessert と it が同一のものなのでここを関係代名詞でつなぎ、it は元の文の目的語なので目的格の関係代名詞 that を使います。

A. Yoona made <u>a Korean dessert</u>.
B. We enjoyed eating <u>it</u>.

➡ We enjoyed eating the Korean dessert <u>that</u> Yoona made.

下の例文の日本語訳を完成させながら使い方を確認しましょう。

Please let me know if there is anything else I can help with.

(   )

Feel free to eat <u>whatever</u> you want.

(   )

> 関係代名詞には先行詞を含むものがあり、what は「〜するもの」、whatever は「〜するものはすべて」となります。

 Let's Listen!   会話の大意を聞き取ろう！

タカシとドナ、ユナの会話を聞いて、質問に対する答えとして最も適切なものを (A)〜(C) の中から1つ選びましょう。 1-75

Question 1   What does Yoona give to Donna?

(A) A non-alcoholic drink
(B) Some dessert she bought
(C) Some cake she made

Question 2   What does Donna say about her husband?

(A) He'll work late tonight.
(B) He's preparing for the meal.
(C) He'll come home soon.

Question 3   What will Takashi probably do next?

(A) Get a non-alcoholic drink for Yoona
(B) Have a seat and make himself at home
(C) Bring some sweets for Donna and Yoona

Let's Check & Read Aloud!

音読してみよう！

1. スクリプトを見ながら会話をもう1度聞き、下線部に当てはまる表現を書き入れましょう。（下線部には単語が2つ入ります）

🎧 1-75

2. 内容を確認して、全文を音読してみましょう。
3. タカシとドナ、ユナの役割をパートナーと一緒に演じてみましょう。

Let's Practice the Roleplay!

Takashi's Role

Yoona's Role

Donna's Role

Takashi introduces his friend, Yoona to his host mother.

Takashi Hi, Donna. Let ①_____ my friend, Yoona. Yoona, this is my host mother, Mrs. Donna Reagan.

Yoona Nice to meet you, Mrs. Reagan.

Donna Nice to meet you too, Yoona. Welcome to our house, and just call me Donna.

Yoona OK, Donna. Thank you for ②_____ this evening. I've heard a ③_____ you from Takashi.

Donna Only good things, I hope.

Takashi You can ④_____ me for that, Donna.

Yoona I've brought you some cake ⑤_____ made. I hope you'll like it.

Donna Oh, thank you so much. Let's have this for dessert. My husband Ron is preparing for a barbecue in the yard now, and he'll be ⑥_____ soon. When it comes to setting up a barbecue, he is the expert. Well, have a seat and ⑦_____ at home, Yoona.

Yoona Thanks.

Takashi Is there anything I can do to help, Donna?

Donna Could you prepare the drinks?

Takashi OK. Can I get you something to drink, Yoona?

Yoona Something non-alcoholic ⑧_____ great, thank you.

ⅿⅿ 音読のヒント ☀

Mrs. Reagan の Mrs. はカタカナ英語の影響で「ミセス」と発音しがちですが、正しくは「ミシィズ」 [mísiz] です。また、会話の中で使われていた that I は、「ザット・アイ」ではなく、「ザライ」のように聞こえます。音がつながるだけなら「ザッタイ」になりそうですが、アメリカ英語では [t] が母音に挟まれた場合、ラ行に近い音になります。

Grammar

文法に強くなろう！

A. 次の文の空所に補うのに適切な関係代名詞をカッコ内から選び○で囲みましょう。

1. I have a friend (who / whose / which) father owns a Korean restaurant near the school.

2. I have a friend (who / whose / which) can sing and dance really well.

3. Thank you. This is just (what / which / that) I wanted.

4. A party is a social occasion (which / at which / whose) people eat, drink, talk, and enjoy themselves.

B. 例にならい、関係代名詞節を用いて2つの文を1つにまとめましょう。出だしが書いてあるものはそれに続く形で文を作りましょう。

例　Yoona gave me a photo. I've lost it.
　　I've lost ___the photo (that) Yoona gave me._____

1. I have an uncle. He lives in Los Angeles.

　　_____

2. The cake is delicious. You made it for us.

　　The cake _____

3. Yoona is going out with a Chinese guy. I can't remember his name.

　　Yoona is going out with a Chinese guy _____

4. Yoona is talking to a girl. Do you know the girl?

　　Do you know the girl _____

C. 日本語の意味に合うようにカッコ内の語句を並べ替え、英文を完成させましょう。ただし、文の始めにくる単語も小文字にしてあり、1つ余分な語句が含まれています。

1. 好きなものは何でも遠慮せずに食べてください。

　　Feel free (to / which / eat / whatever / like / you).

　　_____

2. あそこで料理をしている男性が夫のロンです。

　　(over / whose / who / is / cooking / the man) there is my husband, Ron.

　　_____

3. これは今まで食べた中で1番おいしいです。

　　This is (had / food / what / I've ever / best / the).

　　_____

4. 私に何かお手伝いできることがあれば、お知らせください。

　　Let me know if (anything / can do / is / there / I / are) to help.

　　_____

Let's Read!

次のパッセージを読み、その内容について 1 〜 3 の質問に答えましょう。 1-76

Pounds, Feet and Inches

When you step on <u>a bathroom scale</u> in the U.S., you might be surprised to see that your weight is more than a hundred! Americans measure their weight in pounds (lb). So someone who weighs 75 kilos in Japan will weigh about 165 pounds in the U.S. Measuring height in English-speaking countries may also confuse you. Height is measured in feet and inches. One foot and one inch are equal to 30.48 centimeters and 2.54 centimeters, respectively. Someone who is 168 cm in Japan will be 5 feet 6 inches (5'6") in the U.S. The average height for American men 20 years old and up is about 5 feet 9 inches. Anyone over 6 feet (183 cm) is considered tall.

1. "A bathroom scale" (underlined) will tell you how much you _____.

   (A) weight

   (B) weigh

   (C) weighed

2. One inch is _____ 2.54 cm.

   (A) close to

   (B) longer than

   (C) the same as

3. Which sentence is true?

   (A) The unit for measuring weight in the U.S. is the same as in Japan.

   (B) Measuring your height with U.S. measurement may cause you to feel confused.

   (C) The average height for an American male 20 years old and up is 183 cm.

[Notes]

pound: ポンド（重量単位。記号は lb）　　　confuse: 〜を戸惑わせる
respectively: それぞれ

Challenge Yourself!

Part I PHOTOGRAPHS

(A)～(C) の英文を聞き、写真の描写として最も適切なものを選びましょう。 1-77

1.

    (A)   (B)   (C)

2.

    (A)   (B)   (C)

Part II QUESTION-RESPONSE

最初に聞こえてくる英文に対する応答として最も適切なものを (A)～(C) の中から選びましょう。 1-78

3. (A)   (B)   (C)

4. (A)   (B)   (C)

Part III SHORT CONVERSATIONS

会話を聞き、下の英文が会話の内容と合っていれば T（True）、間違っていれば F（False）を○で囲みましょう。 1-79

5. The man is planning to buy drinks at the restaurant.   T   F

6. The man doesn't enjoy doing the barbecue.   T   F

 Let's Read Aloud & Write!

授業のまとめとして、今日学習した対話文を３回書き写してしっかり覚えましょう。１度英文を声に出して読んでから書き写すと頭に残りやすくなります。

 今日のまとめ

英語で答えられますか？   Do you like barbecues?

UNIT 14 I'd like to pay by credit card.

文法 接続詞・前置詞

帰国の日が迫ってきたある日、タカシは免税品店で買い物をします。会話では、好みを述べたり、意向を尋ねたりする際の表現を学びます。また、文法では**接続詞・前置詞**に焦点を当てて学習します。

Warm-up

授業前に確認しておこう！

≫ Vocabulary Preview

1 ～ 10 の語句の意味として適切なものを a ～ j の中から選びましょう。　🎵 1-80

1. in particular	_____	a.	免税の
2. gift-wrap	_____	b.	価格
3. enter	_____	c.	最新の
4. look for	_____	d.	むしろ～の方を好む
5. regular	_____	e.	～を入力する
6. duty-free	_____	f.	～をプレゼント用に包む
7. prefer	_____	g.	特に、とりわけ
8. showcase	_____	h.	通常の、いつもの
9. latest	_____	i.	陳列箱
10. price	_____	j.	～を探す

ビートに乗って 1 ～ 10 の語句を発音してみましょう。

≫ Grammar Point : 接続詞・前置詞

You'll get a discount <u>if</u> you pay in cash.　　（現金でお支払いでしたら値引きいたします）

I'll text you <u>as soon as</u> I get to the shop.　　（その店に着いたらすぐにメールします）

I'd like to exchange this <u>for</u> another, please.

（これを他のものと交換していただきたいのですが）

　接続詞は様々な語や**句**、**節**などを結びつける役割を果たします。because や if のようによく知られたものの他、as soon as（～したらすぐに）などのように 2 語以上で接続詞的に使われるものもあります。次の表に枠の中から適切な接続詞を書き入れて確認しましょう。

because	～なので	after	～した後で		～しなければ
or	または	before	～する前に		～だけれども
so	それで	when	～するとき		～の場合は
	～の間		～するまで		～である限りは

because ✓
while
although
until
as long as
unless
in case

86

次に、**前置詞**は、<u>in</u> August や <u>on</u> Sunday morning のように、名詞や名詞句の前に置かれ、形容詞や副詞の役割を果たします。前置詞と名詞が一緒になったものを**前置詞句**と呼びます。

接続詞と前置詞では、because と because of、while と during など、意味の似たものがありますので違いを確認しておきましょう。接続詞と前置詞を見分けるポイントは次の通りです。

接続詞	その後に主語と動詞を含む語句（＝**節**）が続く。 ex.）I'd like to exchange this bag for another <u>because</u> the zipper is broken.
前置詞	その後に主語と動詞を含まない語句（＝**句**）が続く。 ex.）The shop was closed earlier than usual <u>because of</u> heavy rain.

下の例文の日本語訳を完成させながら使い方を確認しましょう。

How much discount will there be <u>during</u> the sale?

（　　　　　　　　　　　　　　　　　　　　　　　　　）

I lost my wallet <u>while</u> (I was) shopping at a supermarket.

（　　　　　　　　　　　　　　　　　　　　　　　　　）

 Let's Listen!　　　　　　　　　会話の大意を聞き取ろう！

タカシと店員の会話を聞いて、質問に対する答えとして最も適切なものを(A)～(C)の中から1つ選びましょう。　 1-81

Question 1　Who does Takashi buy the gift for?

(A) For himself

(B) For his father

(C) For his mother

Question 2　What does Takashi ask the clerk to do?

(A) Show him less expensive goods

(B) Give him a discount

(C) Wrap the gift

Question 3　What will Takashi probably do next?

(A) Enter the PIN *

(B) Change the PIN

(C) Apply for a credit card

[Note] PIN: 暗証番号（= personal identification number）

Let's Check & Read Aloud! 音読してみよう！

1. スクリプトを見ながら会話をもう 1 度聞き、下線部に当てはまる表現を書き入れ
   ましょう。（下線部には単語が 2 つ入ります） 1-81
2. 内容を確認して、全文を音読してみましょう。
3. タカシと店員の役割をパートナーと一緒に演じてみましょう。

Let's Practice the Roleplay!

Clerk's Role

Takashi's Role

Takashi is shopping at a duty-free shop.

| Clerk | Are you looking for something in particular? |

| Takashi | Yes, can I take a ①_____ this watch in the showcase? |

| Clerk | Certainly. Here you go. Is this a present for someone or ②_____ ? |

| Takashi | I'm ③_____ a present for my father. |

| Clerk | OK. How about this one? It's the latest model and very popular right now. |

| Takashi | Well, it looks nice, but I prefer the ④_____ . |

| Clerk | I see. |

| Takashi | How much is it? |

| Clerk | It's 190 dollars. This is with a discount of five percent on the ⑤_____ . |

| Takashi | OK. I'll take it. Can you ⑥_____ ? |

| Clerk | Sure. How would you like to ⑦_____ this? |

| Takashi | I'd like to pay by credit card. Here you are. |

| Clerk | Thank you. Please ⑧_____ PIN and press "OK." |

〜〜〜音読のヒント〜

カタカナ英語の影響で showcase や OK を「ショーケース」、「オーケー」のように発音していま
せんか？　特に、カタカナ英語で長音符（ー）を使っている箇所は実際の英語の発音ではそうなら
ない場合が多いので注意しましょう。正しくは、それぞれ「ショウケイス」[ʃóukèis]、「オゥケィ」
[òukéɪ] です。credit card も「クレジットカード」ではなく、「クレディッカード」[krédɪt kàːrd] で、
crédit càrd のように最初の credit に強勢を置きましょう。

 **Grammar** 文法に強くなろう！

A. 例にならい、枠の中から適切な単語を選んで次の 1 ～ 4 の文を完成させましょう。

> 例　I want to look at shoes, (*so*) let's split up.

1. You will never know (　　　　　) you try.

2. I'll go to the store (　　　　　) school is over.

3. Hurry up, (　　　　　) the store will close!

4. It looks great, (　　　　　) I'd like something less expensive.

> | |
> |---|
> | or |
> | but |
> | as soon as |
> | unless |
> | so ✓ |

B. 例にならい、カッコ内から正しい語句を選び○で囲みましょう。

> 例　There is a large shoe store (at / (on)) the second floor.

1. I want to visit this shop again (while / during) my stay in Los Angeles.

2. Let's meet again here (in / at) an hour.

3. All the shops were closed (because / because of) heavy rain.

4. I'll pay (on / in) cash.

C. 日本語の意味に合うようにカッコ内の語句を並べ替え、英文を完成させましょう。ただし、文の始めにくる単語も小文字にしてあり、1 つ余分な語句が含まれています。

1. 私が戻ってくるまでこれをとっておいていただけませんか？

   Could you keep this for (back / I / come / by / until / me)?

   _____

2. これを返品したいのですが。

   I wonder (if / return / you / this / can / I).

   _____

3. このバッグで別の色はありますか？

   Do you have (color / this bag / in / for / a / different)?

   _____

4. 最近はどんな色が流行っていますか？

   (are / in / fashion / what / on / colors) these days?

   _____

次のパッセージを読み、その内容について 1 ～ 3 の質問に答えましょう。 1-82

Money

The major currencies of the world have symbols to identify them. Instead of writing dollars, euros, pounds and yen, we use $, €, £ and ¥. The symbols for the euro and the yen are easy to understand, but why does the pound look like an "L"? And why is the dollar an "S"? The pound is named after the ancient Roman measure of weight, the "libra pondo." A "libra" was a <u>balance</u> used to weigh things. The £ is an L for "libra." The dollar's name comes from an old European coin, the "thaler." But its symbol, $, comes from the combination of the "p" and "s" of the Spanish word "pesos."

1. Which sentence is true?

   (A) Few currencies of the world have symbols.

   (B) The symbols for dollar and pound are very easy to understand.

   (C) It's not easy to see why the symbols for pound and dollar are used.

2. The underlined word "balance" means _____.

   (A) metal

   (B) scale

   (C) stone

3. The symbol for the dollar comes from _____.

   (A) the two letters "p" and "s"

   (B) an old European measure of weight

   (C) the word "thaler"

[Notes]

currency: 貨幣   identify: 見分ける   pound: ポンド（イギリスの貨幣単位）
ancient: 古代の   measure of weight: 重量の単位
thaler: ターラー（ターレルとも言う。15 世紀末から 19 世紀にかけて、ヨーロッパ各地で用いられた銀貨）
pesos: ペソ（中南米諸国およびフィリピンの貨幣単位）
の複数形。イラストが示すように、その省略形で
ある Ps から＄の記号が生まれた。

pesos ➡ Pˢ ➡ 𝕤 ➡ $

Challenge Yourself! リスニング力を試そう！

Part I PHOTOGRAPHS

(A)〜(C) の英文を聞き、写真の描写として最も適切なものを選びましょう。 1-83

1.

   (A)　　　(B)　　　(C)

2.

   (A)　　　(B)　　　(C)

Part II QUESTION-RESPONSE

最初に聞こえてくる英文に対する応答として最も適切なものを（A）〜（C）の中から選びましょう。 1-84

3.　(A)　　　(B)　　　(C)

4.　(A)　　　(B)　　　(C)

Part III SHORT CONVERSATIONS

会話を聞き、下の英文が会話の内容と合っていればT（True）、間違っていればF（False）を○で囲みましょう。 1-85

5. The man should pay 150 dollars.　　　　　　　　　T　　　F

6. The man tries to find change for the hundred-dollar bill.　　T　　　F

 Let's Read Aloud & Write! 音読筆写で覚えよう！

授業のまとめとして、今日学習した対話文を3回書き写してしっかり覚えましょう。1度英文を声に出して読んでから書き写すと頭に残りやすくなります。

今日のまとめ

英語で答えられますか？　　Do you like shopping? How often do you go shopping?

UNIT 15 | I'm looking forward to seeing you again.

文法 動名詞

いよいよ帰国の日、タカシは空港まで見送りに来てくれたドナに感謝の言葉を伝えます。会話では、意思を示したり、話題を変えたりする際の表現を学びます。また、文法では**動名詞**に焦点を当てて学習します。

Warm-up

授業前に確認しておこう！

≫ Vocabulary Preview

1 ～ 10 の語句の意味として適切なものを a ～ j の中から選びましょう。　🎵 1-86

1. appreciate	_____	a.	ところで
2. see ... off	_____	b.	〜を楽しみに待つ
3. spend	_____	c.	〜を見送る
4. someday	_____	d.	いつか
5. give one's best to	_____	e.	具体的な
6. all the way	_____	f.	感謝する
7. by the way	_____	g.	（時間）を費やす
8. anytime	_____	h.	〜する時はいつでも
9. specific	_____	i.	〜によろしくと伝える
10. look forward to	_____	j.	（遠路）はるばる

ビートに乗って 1 ～ 10 の語句を発音してみましょう。

≫ Grammar Point : 動名詞

<u>Seeing</u> is <u>believing</u>.　　（見ることは信じること⇒百聞は一見に如かず）［主語や補語になる］

I enjoyed <u>visiting</u> a lot of places with you.

　　　　（あなたといろんな場所を訪ねることができて楽しかったです）［動詞の目的語になる］

Thank you for <u>coming</u> here to see me off.

　　　　　　（見送りに来てくださりありがとうございます）［前置詞の目的語になる］

　動詞の ing 形は現在分詞として「〜している」という意味で使われますが、それとは別に「〜すること」のように動詞を名詞化する場合にも使われ、これを**動名詞**と言います。動詞が名詞の働きをするものには to 不定詞もありますが、3 番目の例文のように前置詞の後には to 不定詞ではなく必ず動名詞を使います。この他にも動名詞と to 不定詞には注意すべき用法がありますので、次の表で確認しましょう。

必ず動名詞を目的語とする動詞	enjoy, finish, mind, stop, suggest, etc.
必ず to 不定詞を目的語とする動詞	expect, hope, learn, mean, want, etc.
どちらも目的語とする動詞	begin, like, love, start, etc.
動名詞か to 不定詞かで 意味が異なる動詞	forget, remember, try, etc. 動名詞は「すでに起きたこと」、to 不定詞は「これから先のこと」 と覚えておくとよいでしょう。 ex.）I'll never <u>forget visiting</u> this city.　（～したことを忘れる） ex.）Don't <u>forget to call</u> us when you get there. （～し忘れる）

また、下の表に挙げる表現では動名詞がよく使われます。

be used to ...	～に慣れている
feel like ...	～したい気がする
How about ...?	～してはどうですか
Would you mind ...?	～していただけませんか

下の例文の日本語訳を完成させながら使い方を確認しましょう。

I'm used to <u>introducing</u> myself in English now.

（　　　　　　　　　　　　　　　　　　　　　　　　　　　）

Would you mind <u>taking</u> our picture?

（　　　　　　　　　　　　　　　　　　　　　　　　　　　）

Let's Listen!　　　　　　　会話の大意を聞き取ろう！

タカシとドナの会話を聞いて、質問に対する答えとして最も適切なものを（A）～（C） 1-87
の中から１つ選びましょう。

Question 1　　What does Takashi ask Donna to do?

(A) Help him carry his luggage

(B) Say hello to Ron for him

(C) Look forward to seeing him again

Question 2　　Does Donna have any plans to visit Japan?

(A) Yes, she's going to visit Kyoto next year.

(B) No, but Ron will visit Kyoto next year.

(C) Not at the moment, but she wants to visit Japan someday.

Question 3　　What does Takashi suggest?

(A) He should stay at Donna's house again.

(B) Ron and Donna should visit Kyoto.

(C) Ron and Donna should stay at his house when they visit Japan.

Let's Check & Read Aloud! 音読してみよう！

1. スクリプトを見ながら会話をもう１度聞き、下線部に当てはまる表現を書き入れ 1-87
   ましょう。（下線部には単語が２つ入ります）
2. 内容を確認して、全文を音読してみましょう。
3. タカシとドナの役割をパートナーと一緒に演じてみましょう。

Let's Practice the Roleplay!

Takashi's Role   Donna's Role

Takashi and Donna are at the airport.

Takashi　Thank you for coming all the way to see ①＿＿＿＿＿＿＿＿＿ at the airport.

Donna　My pleasure.

Takashi　I ②＿＿＿＿＿＿＿＿＿ you did for me during my stay here. I had a really good time.

Donna　Oh, don't mention it. Ron and I enjoyed ③＿＿＿＿＿＿＿＿＿ with you, too.

Takashi　Please remember to give ④＿＿＿＿＿＿＿＿＿ to him.

Donna　OK, I will. He says that there are still a lot of places that he wanted to take you to.

Takashi　Uh-huh. By the way, do you have any plans to visit Japan? I'd like ⑤＿＿＿＿＿＿＿＿＿ the favor.

Donna　Well, we don't have any ⑥＿＿＿＿＿＿＿＿＿ right now, but we want to visit Kyoto someday.

Takashi　Please stay with us anytime you're there. My family ⑦＿＿＿＿＿＿＿＿＿ very happy to see you.

Donna　Thank you. I'm looking forward ⑧＿＿＿＿＿＿＿＿＿ you again.

〰️音読のヒント 💡

uh-huh は、「うん、ええ、そうですか」のように、同意やあいづちに使われる表現ですが、発音はなかなか難しいです。鼻にかけた感じの「アハァ」[əhʌ́] で、後の「ハァ」の部分は上がり調子になります。

A. 例にならい、枠の中から適切な単語を選び、動名詞か to 不定詞にして次の 1 〜 4 の文を完成させましょう。

| speak |
| look |
| hear |
| visit |
| call ✓ |

例 Thank you for (*calling*) me.

1. I need to practice (　　　　　) English more.

2. Thanks for (　　　　　) after me. I enjoyed staying here a lot.

3. I hope (　　　　　) Paris sometime.

4. I look forward to (　　　　　) from you.

B. 例にならい、カッコ内から正しい語句を選び○で囲みましょう。

例 Donna wants ((to visit) / visiting) Kyoto someday.

1. What are good things about (to go / going) abroad?

2. I'd like (to see / see) you again.

3. My friends don't worry about (make / making) mistakes in class.

4. "I have to pack my suitcase." "Don't forget (to weigh / weighing) it."

C. 日本語の意味に合うようにカッコ内の語句を並べ替え、英文を完成させましょう。ただし、文の始めにくる単語も小文字にしてあり、1 つ余分な語句が含まれています。

1. 日本に帰る用意はできていますか？

(ready / go / going / you / to / are) back to Japan?

_____

2. スーツケースを詰め始める必要があります。

(start / to / packing / pack / I / need) my suitcase.

_____

3. 忘れずに私たちにメールしてください。

(e-mail / e-mailing / don't / to / us / forget).

_____

4. 私はロサンゼルスを訪れたことを決して忘れません。

(forget / I'll / never / visiting / to visit / Los Angeles).

_____

 **Let's Read!**

次のカードを読み、その内容について１～３の質問に答えましょう。　 1-88

A Thank-You Card

Dear Ron and Donna,

This is just a short message to thank you for all the kindness and <u>hospitality</u> that you showed me over the past four weeks. I had such a good time with you, and I'll never forget the memories that I've shared with you and your family.

I enjoyed talking with you and learning about America. Your cooking was great, and everyone was so kind to me. I really feel like San Bernardino is my second home!

If you're ever in Japan, please let me know. I'd love to introduce you to my family and show you my home and culture.

Thanks so much again.

Love,

Takashi

1. Showing someone "hospitality" (underlined) means making them feel _____.

   (A) convenient

   (B) tired

   (C) welcome

2. Which sentence is true?

   (A) Takashi wants to introduce Ron and Donna to his family.

   (B) Takashi is thinking of buying a second home in the U.S.

   (C) Takashi apologizes for not being able to eat Donna's food.

3. Takashi stayed with Ron and Donna for _____.

   (A) less than three weeks

   (B) about a month

   (C) four months

Challenge Yourself! リスニング力を試そう！

Part I PHOTOGRAPHS

（A）～（C）の英文を聞き、写真の描写として最も適切なものを選びましょう。 1-89

1.

（A）　　（B）　　（C）

2.

（A）　　（B）　　（C）

Part II QUESTION-RESPONSE

最初に聞こえてくる英文に対する応答として最も適切なものを（A）～（C）の中 1-90
から選びましょう。

3.　（A）　　　（B）　　　（C）

4.　（A）　　　（B）　　　（C）

Part III SHORT CONVERSATIONS

会話を聞き、下の英文が会話の内容と合っていれば T（True）、間違っていれば 1-91
F（False）を○で囲みましょう。

5. The man has planned a visit to Osaka.　　　　　　　　　　T　　　　F

6. The man is happy to be going home.　　　　　　　　　　T　　　　F

 Let's Read Aloud & Write! 音読筆写で覚えよう！

授業のまとめとして、今日学習した対話文を3回書き写して
しっかり覚えましょう。1度英文を声に出して読んでから書き
写すと頭に残りやすくなります。

今日のまとめ

英語で答えられますか？　　　Do you have any plans to visit the United States?

UNIT 01 *Let's Review!*　　　　　しっかり復習しよう！

》Quick Response Training　　　　 2-01

1. 日本語の文と同じ意味を表すようにカッコ内に適切な単語を入れて英文を完成させましょう。
2. 日本語の文を見てすぐさま対応する英文が言えるように繰り返し練習しましょう。英文の箇所を隠して練習すると効果的です。
3. 1〜10 までの日本語の文を何秒で英文にして言えるかペアで競い合ってみましょう。

Your Time: 〈　　〉 seconds

1. これが私の搭乗券です。	1. (　　　) is my boarding pass.
2. これは私が機内に持ち込む荷物です。	2. This (　　) my carry-on bag.
3. すみません。そこは私の席だと思います（あなたは私の席にいると思います）。	3. Excuse me. I think you (　　) in my seat.
4. 日本を訪れるのはこれが初めてですか？	4. (　　　) this your first visit to Japan?
5. あれは私のスーツケースではありません。	5. That (　　) my suitcase.
6. 手荷物受取所はどこですか？	6. Where (　　) the baggage claim area?
7. 両替所はどこですか？	7. (　　) is the exchange counter?
8. 空の旅はいかがでしたか？	8. How (　　) the flight?
9. そこの現地時間は何時ですか？	9. (　　) is the local time there?
10.【機内で】機内に日本の新聞はありますか？	10. (　　) there any Japanese newspapers on board?

》Linguaporta Training

授業の復習として、リンガポルタの問題を解いておきましょう。
次回授業の始めに復習テストがあります。

UNIT 02 — Let's Review!

しっかり復習しよう！

>> Quick Response Training

 2-02

1. 日本語の文と同じ意味を表すようにカッコ内に適切な単語を入れて英文を完成させましょう。
2. 日本語の文を見てすぐさま対応する英文が言えるように繰り返し練習しましょう。英文の箇所を隠して練習すると効果的です。
3. 1〜10 までの日本語の文を何秒で英文にして言えるかペアで競い合ってみましょう。

Your Time: 〈　　　〉 **seconds**

1. 【機内で】日本の新聞はありますか？	1. (　　　) you have any Japanese newspapers?
2. 【機内で】食事は必要ではありません。	2. I (　　　) need a meal.
3. 【税関で】何か申告するものはありますか？	3. (　　　) you have anything to declare?
4. 【税関で】申告するものは何もありません。	4. I (　　　) have anything to declare.
5. 私たちはよく海外旅行に行きます。	5. We (　　　) travel abroad.
6. 父は旅行が好きではありません。	6. My father (　　　) like to travel.
7. 祖母は決して飛行機に乗りません。	7. My grandmother (　　　) flies.
8. お仕事は何ですか？	8. What (　　　) you do?
9. 日本はいかがですか？	9. (　　　) do you like Japan?
10. 毎年、夏休みには家族で旅行します。	10. Every year my family (　　　) on a trip during summer vacation.

>> Linguaporta Training

授業の復習として、リンガポルタの問題を解いておきましょう。
次回授業の始めに復習テストがあります。

UNIT 03 Let's Review!

しっかり復習しよう！

 2-03

1. 日本語の文と同じ意味を表すようにカッコ内に適切な単語を入れて英文を完成させましょう。
2. 日本語の文を見てすぐさま対応する英文が言えるように繰り返し練習しましょう。英文の箇所を隠して練習すると効果的です。
3. 1〜10 までの日本語の文を何秒で英文にして言えるかペアで競い合ってみましょう。

Your Time: ⬡ **seconds**

1. （私は）旅行のために新しいスーツケースを買いました。	1. I ( ) a new suitcase for my trip.
2. どこでそれを買いましたか？	2. Where ( ) you buy it?
3. 父が空港まで車で送ってくれました。	3. My father ( ) me a ride to the airport.
4. 入国審査ではとても苦労しました。	4. I ( ) a lot of trouble at immigration.
5. どれくらい（の時間）待ちましたか？	5. How ( ) did you wait?
6. 空の旅は良かったですか（あなたは良い空の旅を持ちましたか）？	6. ( ) you have a good flight?
7. 機内ではよく眠れませんでした。	7. I ( ) sleep well <u>on the plane</u>.
8. いつハワイに行ったのですか？	8. ( ) did you go to Hawaii?
9. 昨年の夏、家族とハワイに行きました。	9. I ( ) to Hawaii with my family last summer.
10. どれくらいの頻度で海外旅行に出かけますか？	10. How ( ) do you travel abroad?

≫ *Linguaporta Training*

授業の復習として、リンガポルタの問題を解いておきましょう。
次回授業の始めに復習テストがあります。

UNIT 04 Let's Review!

しっかり復習しよう！

» Quick Response Training

 2-04

1. 日本語の文と同じ意味を表すようにカッコ内に適切な単語を入れて英文を完成させましょう。
2. 日本語の文を見てすぐさま対応する英文が言えるように繰り返し練習しましょう。英文の箇所を隠して練習すると効果的です。
3. 1〜10 までの日本語の文を何秒で英文にして言えるかペアで競い合ってみましょう。

Your Time: ⬡ seconds

1. 【呼ばれた際に】今（そちらに）行きます。	1. I'm ( ).
2. 今、シャワー中です。	2. I'm ( ) a shower now.
3. 誰かここに座っていますか（この席、どなたかいらっしゃいますか）？	3. Is someone ( ) here?
4. どこに行くのですか（どこに行くところなのですか）？	4. Where are you ( )?
5. どうしてここにいるのですか（ここで何しているのですか）？	5. What ( ) you doing here?
6. 体調があまり良くありません。	6. I'm ( ) feeling very well.
7. 電話してくれた時は寝ていました。	7. I ( ) sleeping when you called me.
8. もう寝ます。	8. I'm ( ) to bed.
9. 今朝起きた時、雨は降っていませんでした。	9. It ( ) raining when I got up this morning.
10. いいレストランを知っていますよ。	10. I ( ) a good restaurant.

» Linguaporta Training

授業の復習として、リンガポルタの問題を解いておきましょう。
次回授業の始めに復習テストがあります。

Quick Response Training

 2-05

1. 日本語の文と同じ意味を表すようにカッコ内に適切な単語を入れて英文を完成させましょう。
2. 日本語の文を見てすぐさま対応する英文が言えるように繰り返し練習しましょう。英文の箇所を隠して練習すると効果的です。
3. 1〜10までの日本語の文を何秒で英文にして言えるかペアで競い合ってみましょう。

Your Time: ⬡ **seconds**

1. 【席を外す際に】すぐに戻ります。	1. (　　　) be right back.
2. 【席を外す際に】長くはかかりません（すぐに戻ります）。	2. I (　　　) be long.
3. 放課後何をする予定ですか？	3. What (　　　) you going to do after school?
4. プレゼンの準備をする予定です。	4. I'm going (　　　) prepare for my presentation.
5. ビジネス英語のコースを取る予定ですか？	5. (　　　) you going to take a course in Business English?
6. コンピューターのコースを取るつもりはありません。	6. I'm (　　　) going to take a course in computers.
7. 【ホームステイ先で】私が食器を洗います。	7. (　　　) wash the dishes.
8. 【ホームステイ先で】明日は8時に出かけるつもりです。	8. (　　　) going to leave at eight o'clock tomorrow.
9. 【ホームステイ先で】夕食までには家に帰ります。	9. (　　　) be home by dinner.
10. 【ホームステイ先で】あなたが日本にお越しの際は私が案内します。	10. I'll show you around when (　　　) come to Japan.

Linguaporta Training

授業の復習として、リンガポルタの問題を解いておきましょう。
次回授業の始めに復習テストがあります。

Let's Review!

しっかり復習しよう！

≫ Quick Response Training

 2-06

1. 日本語の文と同じ意味を表すようにカッコ内に適切な単語を入れて英文を完成させましょう。
2. 日本語の文を見てすぐさま対応する英文が言えるように繰り返し練習しましょう。英文の箇所を隠して練習すると効果的です。
3. 1〜10までの日本語の文を何秒で英文にして言えるかペアで競い合ってみましょう。

Your Time: 〈　〉 seconds

1. この席は誰か座っていますか？	1. (　　　) this seat taken?
2. 英語は世界中で話されています。	2. English is (　　　) around the world.
3. 私の自転車が昨日盗まれました。	3. My bicycle was (　　　) yesterday.
4. 明日、歓迎会が開かれる予定です。	4. A welcome party (　　　) be held tomorrow.
5. ブラウン先生*1は学生全員から愛されています。	5. Mr. Brown (　　　) loved by all the students.
6. 学生は皆、ブラウン先生の授業が大好きです。	6. All the students (　　　) Mr. Brown's class.
7. ブラウン先生は昨日授業を休講にしました。	7. Mr. Brown (　　　) his class yesterday.
8. 理由は私たちに明かされませんでした（理由は私たちに与えられませんでした）。	8. No reason (　　　) given to us.
9. エアコンは現在、修理中です。	9. The air conditioner (　　　) being repaired now.
10. トイレ*2は現在、清掃中です。	10. The restroom is (　　　) cleaned now.

[NOTES]
1. 男性であると仮定し、Mr. Brown としましょう。女性の場合は、Ms. Brown のように、Ms.（ミズ）を使います。
2. 公共の場所などの場合は restroom を使い、個人宅の場合は bathroom を使います。

≫ Linguaporta Training

授業の復習として、リンガポルタの問題を解いておきましょう。
次回授業の始めに復習テストがあります。

UNIT 07 Let's Review! しっかり復習しよう！

1. 日本語の文と同じ意味を表すようにカッコ内に適切な単語を入れて英文を完成させましょう。
2. 日本語の文を見てすぐさま対応する英文が言えるように繰り返し練習しましょう。英文の箇所を隠して練習すると効果的です。
3. 1～10 までの日本語の文を何秒で英文にして言えるかペアで競い合ってみましょう。

Your Time: ⬡ **seconds**

1. 2 人用の席をお願いします。	1. I'd*1 (　　　) a table for two, please.
2. 窓際の席をお願いします。	2. (　　　) like a table by the window, please.
3. メニューを見せていただけますか？	3. Can (　　　) see the menu?
4. 【注文で】もう少し時間をいただけますか？	4. Could*2 (　　　) wait a few minutes?
5. 【注文で】あなたと同じものにします。	5. I'll have the (　　　) as you.
6. 【注文で】これにします。	6. (　　　) have this one.
7. お水をいただけますか？	7. Could (　　　) get me some water?
8. （お皿を指さしながら）これを下げていただけますか？	8. Could (　　　) take this away, please?
9. お手洗いはどこでしょうか（どこで手を洗うことができますか）？	9. Where can (　　　) wash my hands?
10. 予約をする必要はありません。	10. You (　　　) have to make a reservation.

[NOTES]
1. 連れの人のことを意識して We'd ということも可能です。2 についても同様です。
2. can も可能ですが、could を使うと丁寧な感じになります。

》 Linguaporta Training

　授業の復習として、リンガポルタの問題を解いておきましょう。

次回授業の始めに復習テストがあります。

>> **Quick Response Training**　　　 2-08

1. 日本語の文と同じ意味を表すようにカッコ内に適切な単語を入れて英文を完成させましょう。
2. 日本語の文を見てすぐさま対応する英文が言えるように繰り返し練習しましょう。英文の箇所を隠して練習すると効果的です。
3. 1〜10までの日本語の文を何秒で英文にして言えるかペアで競い合ってみましょう。

Your Time: ⬡ **seconds**

1.（私は）先月 1 週間入院しました。	1. I （　　　　） in the hospital for a week last month.
2.（私は）入院して 1 週間になります。	2. （　　　　） been in the hospital for a week.
3.（私は）風邪をひいてしまいました。	3. I've caught a （　　　　）.
4.（私は）昨日からずっと高熱が続いています。	4. I've had a high fever （　　　　） yesterday.
5. いつから具合が悪いのですか（どれくらいの間この問題を抱えているのですか）？	5. How long （　　　　） you had this problem?
6. いつこの薬を飲みましたか？	6. When （　　　　） you take this medicine?
7. 久しぶりですね。	7. I （　　　　） seen you for a long time.
8.（あなたは）少しも変わっていませんね。	8. You （　　　　） changed at all.
9. この便は欠航になりました。	9. This flight （　　　　） been canceled.
10. この便は遅れています。	10. This flight has （　　　　） delayed.

>> **Linguaporta Training**

授業の復習として、リンガポルタの問題を解いておきましょう。
次回授業の始めに復習テストがあります。

》》 *Quick Response Training*

 2-09

1. 日本語の文と同じ意味を表すようにカッコ内に適切な単語を入れて英文を完成させましょう。
2. 日本語の文を見てすぐさま対応する英文が言えるように繰り返し練習しましょう。英文の箇所を隠して練習すると効果的です。
3. 1〜10までの日本語の文を何秒で英文にして言えるかペアで競い合ってみましょう。

Your Time: ⬡ **seconds**

1. 私は方向音痴です（私は方向感覚がほとんどありません）。	1. I have ( ) sense of direction.
2. 私はよく道に迷います。	2. I often get ( ).
3. 私はよくグーグル・マップを使います。	3. I ( ) use Google Maps.
4. 私は地図を読むのが得意です。	4. I'm ( ) at reading maps.
5. 私は地図を読むのが苦手です（得意ではありません）。	5. I'm ( ) good at reading maps.
6. 私はその地域をほとんど知りません。	6. I ( ) know the area.
7. 私たちは間違った方向に進んでいます。	7. We're going ( ) the wrong direction.
8. 私たちは電車を間違えました（私たちは間違った電車に乗りました）。	8. We took the ( ) train.
9. （私たちは）時間があまりないから、急ぎましょう。	9. We don't have ( ) time, so let's hurry.
10. 私たちはもう少しでバスに乗り遅れるところでした。	10. We ( ) missed the bus.

》》 *Linguaporta Training*

授業の復習として、リンガポルタの問題を解いておきましょう。
次回授業の始めに復習テストがあります。

UNIT 10 Let's Review!

しっかり復習しよう！

» Quick Response Training

 2-10

1. 日本語の文と同じ意味を表すようにカッコ内に適切な単語を入れて英文を完成させましょう。
2. 日本語の文を見てすぐさま対応する英文が言えるように繰り返し練習しましょう。英文の箇所を隠して練習すると効果的です。
3. 1〜10 までの日本語の文を何秒で英文にして言えるかペアで競い合ってみましょう。

Your Time: ⬡ **seconds**

1. またお会いできてうれしいです。	1. It's nice (　　　) see you again.
2. ここで写真を撮っても大丈夫ですか？	2. Is it OK to (　　　) pictures here?
3. あなたにお願いがあります。	3. I have a favor to (　　　) you.
4. あなたにお話したいことがあります。	4. I have something to (　　　) you.
5. 何か飲み物はいかがですか？	5. Would you like something to (　　　)？
6. あの女性に私たちの写真を撮ってもらうよう頼みましょう。	6. Let's (　　　) that woman to take our picture.
7. お邪魔してすみませんが、私たちの写真を撮っていただけませんでしょうか？	7. I'm sorry (　　　) bother you, but could you take our picture?
8. 私に何をしてほしいのですか？	8. What do you want (　　　) to do?
9. どうしたらいいのかわかりません（何をしたらよいのかわかりません）。	9. I don't know (　　　) to do.
10. このカメラの使い方をあなたにお見せしましょう。	10. I'll show you (　　　) to use this camera.

» Linguaporta Training

授業の復習として、リンガポルタの問題を解いておきましょう。
次回授業の始めに復習テストがあります。

UNIT 11 Let's Review!

しっかり復習しよう！

» Quick Response Training

 2-11

1. 日本語の文と同じ意味を表すようにカッコ内に適切な単語を入れて英文を完成させましょう。
2. 日本語の文を見てすぐさま対応する英文が言えるように繰り返し練習しましょう。英文の箇所を隠して練習すると効果的です。
3. 1〜10までの日本語の文を何秒で英文にして言えるかペアで競い合ってみましょう。

Your Time: ＜　　　＞ seconds

1. 遺失物取扱所はどこですか？	1. Where is the Lost and (　　　) office?
2. その博物館は本当に退屈でした。	2. The museum was really (　　　).
3. （あなたは）退屈なのですか？	3. Are you (　　　)?
4. 兄は私を退屈な奴だとよく言います。	4. My brother often says I'm (　　　).
5. お待たせしてすみませんでした。	5. I'm sorry to keep you (　　　).
6. 私の財布が盗まれました。	6. My wallet was (　　　).
7. 私はパスポートを盗まれました。	7. I had my passport (　　　).
8. 私のスーツケースが行方不明です。	8. My suitcase is (　　　).
9. ドアの前に立っている女性は誰ですか？	9. Who is the woman (　　　) in front of the door?
10. あそこに座っている男性を知っていますか？	10. Do you know the man (　　　) over there?

» Linguaporta Training

授業の復習として、リンガポルタの問題を解いておきましょう。
次回授業の始めに復習テストがあります。

Let's Review!

しっかり復習しよう！

》 Quick Response Training

 2-12

1. 日本語の文と同じ意味を表すようにカッコ内に適切な単語を入れて英文を完成させましょう。
2. 日本語の文を見てすぐさま対応する英文が言えるように繰り返し練習しましょう。英文の箇所を隠して練習すると効果的です。
3. 1〜10までの日本語の文を何秒で英文にして言えるかペアで競い合ってみましょう。

Your Time: ⬡ **seconds**

1. この乗り物はジェットコースターと同じくらい怖いです。	1. This ride is (　　　) scary as the roller coaster.
2. この乗り物はジェットコースターよりも興奮します。	2. This ride is (　　　) exciting than the roller coaster.
3. これはここにある乗り物の中で1番人気があります。	3. This is the (　　　) popular of all the rides here.
4. 今1番人気がある乗り物は何ですか？	4. What is (　　　) most popular ride now?
5. これは予想していたより面白いです。	5. This is more fun (　　　) I expected.
6. これは予想していたほど面白くはないです。	6. This isn't as much fun (　　　) I expected.
7. これは今まで経験した中で1番興奮する乗り物です。	7. This is (　　　) most exciting ride (that) I've ever experienced.
8.【買い物で】もっと安くしてくださいませんか（もっと良い値段を提示してくださいませんか）？	8. Could you give me a (　　　) price?
9.【買い物で】もう少し安いものが欲しいです。	9. I'd like something (　　　) expensive.
10.【買い物で】これでもっと小さいサイズのものはありますか？	10. Do you have this in a (　　　) size?

》 Linguaporta Training

授業の復習として、リンガポルタの問題を解いておきましょう。
次回授業の始めに復習テストがあります。

UNIT 13 Let's Review!

しっかり復習しよう！

>> *Quick Response Training*

 2-13

1. 日本語の文と同じ意味を表すようにカッコ内に適切な単語を入れて英文を完成させましょう。
2. 日本語の文を見てすぐさま対応する英文が言えるように繰り返し練習しましょう。英文の箇所を隠して練習すると効果的です。
3. 1〜10 までの日本語の文を何秒で英文にして言えるかペアで競い合ってみましょう。

Your Time: 〈　　〉 **seconds**

1. 私と一緒に歌ってくれる人が必要です。	1. I need someone <u>who</u> *1 can (　　　) with me.
2. 私には SNS に詳しい友人がいます。	2. I have a friend (　　　) knows a lot about social media.
3. 私たちは築 100 年のホテルでパーティをしました。	3. We had a party at a hotel <u>that</u> *2 was 100 years (　　　).
4. 私には母親が有名な歌手である友人がいます。	4. I have a friend (　　　) mother is a famous singer.
5. 何でも好きなものを注文してください。	5. Order (　　　) (<u>that</u>) *3 you like.
6. 何か必要なものがあれば言ってください。	6. If there is anything (<u>that</u>) (　　　) need, just let me know.
7. 何か私にできることがありますか？	7. Is (　　　) anything (<u>that</u>) I can do?
8. こんなにおいしい食事をいただいたのは初めてです（これは私が今まで食べた中で最高の食事です）。	8. This is the best meal (<u>that</u>) I've (　　　) had.
9. これは私がちょうど欲しかったものです。	9. This is just (　　　) I wanted.
10. 欲しいものは何でも<u>遠慮せずに召し上がって</u>ください。	10. <u>Feel free to eat</u> (　　　) you want. = anything (that)

[NOTES]
1. 先行詞が人で主格の場合、that も可能ですが、who を使うのが一般的です。
2. 先行詞が人以外で主格の場合、which も可能ですが that を使うのが一般的です。
3. 先行詞が目的格の場合省略することが多いですが、使うとすれば先行詞が人かどうかに関わらず that を使うのが一般的です。

>> *Linguaporta Training*

　授業の復習として、リンガポルタの問題を解いておきましょう。

次回授業の始めに復習テストがあります。

UNIT 14 Let's Review!

しっかり復習しよう！

≫ Quick Response Training

1. 日本語の文と同じ意味を表すようにカッコ内に適切な単語を入れて英文を完成させましょう。
2. 日本語の文を見てすぐさま対応する英文が言えるように繰り返し練習しましょう。英文の箇所を隠して練習すると効果的です。
3. 1〜10 までの日本語の文を何秒で英文にして言えるかペアで競い合ってみましょう。

Your Time: ⬡ seconds

1. これと同じもので他の色はありますか？	1. Do you have this (　　　) a different color?
2. 現金で支払います。	2. I'll pay (　　　) cash.
3. セールの間、どのくらい値引きがあるのですか？	3. How much discount will there be (　　　) the sale?
4. 買い物を済ませるまでここで待ってもらえませんか？	4. Could you wait here (　　　) I finish shopping?
5. 2時間後にここで会いましょう。	5. Let's meet here (　　　) two hours.
6. このカバンはセールで買いました。	6. I bought this bag (　　　) sale.
7. （私は）11 時までに家に戻らないといけません。	7. I have to be home (　　　) 11 o'clock.
8. 出発前にもう1度お会いできたらと思います。	8. I hope to see you again (　　　) I go.
9. ご両親によろしく伝えてください。	9. Say hello to your parents (　　　) me.
10. 急いでください。さもないと、（あなたは）飛行機に乗り遅れますよ。	10. Hurry up, (　　　) you'll miss your flight.

≫ Linguaporta Training

授業の復習として、リンガポルタの問題を解いておきましょう。
次回授業の始めに復習テストがあります。

UNIT 15 Let's Review!

≫ Quick Response Training

 2-15

1. 日本語の文と同じ意味を表すようにカッコ内に適切な単語を入れて英文を完成させましょう。
2. 日本語の文を見てすぐさま対応する英文が言えるように繰り返し練習しましょう。英文の箇所を隠して練習すると効果的です。
3. 1〜10 までの日本語の文を何秒で英文にして言えるかペアで競い合ってみましょう。

Your Time: ⬡ **seconds**

1. 【ホームステイ先で】あなたの家族の一員にしてくださりありがとうございます。	1. Thank you (　　　) having me in your family.
2. お話しできて良かったです。	2. It was nice (　　　) to you.
3. たくさんのお力添えをありがとうございました。	3. I want (　　　) thank you for all your help.
4. あなたにまたお会いできるのを楽しみにしています。	4. I'm looking forward (　　　) seeing you again.
5. お待たせしてすみません。	5. I'm sorry to (　　　) you waiting.
6. 遅くなってすみません。	6. I'm sorry for (　　　) late.
7. 今まで連絡できなくてすみません。	7. I'm sorry for (　　　) keeping in touch.
8. おかけになりませんか？	8. Would you like to (　　　) down?
9. ここで勉強したことは決して忘れません。	9. I'll never forget (　　　) here.
10. 忘れずに電話してください。	10. Don't (　　　) to call me.

≫ Linguaporta Training

　授業の復習として、リンガポルタの問題を解いておきましょう。次回授業の始めに復習テストがあります。

巻末資料

品詞の分類

名詞や動詞といった文法上の区分のことを**品詞**と言い、一般に下のように分類されます。

品　詞	働　き	例
名詞（Noun）	人や物事の名前を表す。	company, sale など
冠詞（Article）	名詞の前に置かれて、その単語が特定されるものかどうかを示す。	a, an, the
代名詞（Pronoun）	名詞の代わりをする。	I, my, me, mine など
動詞（Verb）	人や物事の状態や動作を表す。	want, keep, take など
助動詞（Auxiliary verb）	動詞と組み合わせて話し手の判断を示す。	can, will, must など
形容詞（Adjective）	人や物事の性質や状態などを表す。	big, beautiful など
副詞（Adverb）	動詞や形容詞、他の副詞などを修飾する。	really, always など
前置詞（Preposition）	名詞や名詞句の前に置かれ句を作る。	of, in, under, on など
接続詞（Conjunction）	語と語、句と句、節と節をつなぐ。	and, because, or など
間投詞（Interjection）	話し手の感情を表す。	oh, wow, ouch など

単語は必ずしも１つの品詞でしか使われないわけではありません。意味のわからない単語を辞書で引く場合、その単語の品詞が何であるかをあらかじめ考えておくと、正しい意味に早くたどり着けるようになります。

文の要素と基本文型

英文を構成する要素には次のようなものがあります。

主　語	文の中で「〜が、〜は」に当たるもの。	名詞、代名詞
述語動詞	文の中で「〜である」や「〜する」に当たるもの。	動詞
目的語	「〜を」や「〜に」など、動作の対象を示すもの。	名詞、代名詞
補　語	主語や目的語が「どういうものか」もしくは「どんな状態なのか」を補足説明するもの。 ex. My name is Robert, but everyone calls me Bob. （私の名前はロバートですが、みんな私のことをボブと呼びます）	名詞、代名詞、形容詞
修飾語（句）	主語、述語動詞、目的語、補語に意味を付け加えるもの。 修飾語（句）を除いても文は成立します。 ex. I work for Sunrise Corporation. （私はサンライズ・コーポレーションに勤めています）	形容詞、副詞、前置詞句など

また、英文の基本文型としては下に挙げる **5 文型** がよく知られています。

第 1 文型	SV （主語 ＋ 動詞）	I cried.（私は泣いた）
第 2 文型	SVC （主語 ＋ 動詞 ＋ 補語）	My name is Robert.（私の名前はロバートです）
第 3 文型	SVO （主語 ＋ 動詞 ＋ 目的語）	I studied economics.（私は経済学を学びました）
第 4 文型	SVO_1O_2 （主語 ＋ 動詞 ＋ 目的語 1 ＋ 目的語 2）	Julia gave me the report. （ジュリアが私にその報告書をくれました）
第 5 文型	SVOC （主語 ＋ 動詞 ＋ 目的語 ＋ 補語）	Everybody calls me Bob. （みんな私のことをボブと呼びます）

　主語（Subject）、**述語動詞**（Verb）、**目的語**（Object）、**補語**（Complement）という基本要素の中で、目的語と補語の区別が文型を見分けるポイントになります。目的語は動詞が表す動作の対象を示し、補語は主語や目的語が「どういうものか」もしくは「どんな状態なのか」を補足説明するものです。ですから、第 2 文型と第 3 文型を見分ける場合、**「第 2 文型の場合 S ＝ C、第 3 文型の場合 S ≠ O」** という関係に着目するとよいでしょう。また、第 4 文型と第 5 文型を見分ける場合には、**「第 4 文型の場合 O_1 ≠ O_2、第 5 文型の場合 O ＝ C」** という関係が成り立つことに注意しておくことです。

▰▰ 人称代名詞の種類と格変化表 ▰▰

人称	数	主格 （～は）	所有格 （～の）	目的格 （～に、～を）	所有代名詞 （～のもの）	再帰代名詞 （～自身）
1 人称	単数	I	my	me	mine	myself
	複数	we	our	us	ours	ourselves
2 人称	単数	you	your	you	yours	yourself
	複数					yourselves
3 人称	単数	he	his	him	his	himself
		she	her	her	hers	herself
		it	its	it	－	itself
	複数	they	their	them	theirs	themselves

▰ 不規則動詞変化表 ▰

	原　形	過去形	過去分詞形	-ing 形	
A-A-A （原形、過去形、過去分詞が すべて同じ）	cost cut hit put read	cost cut hit put read [réd]	cost cut hit put read [réd]	costing cutting hitting putting reading	（費用が）かかる 切る 叩く 置く 読む
A-B-A （原形と過去 分詞が同じ）	become come run	became came ran	become come run	becoming coming running	〜になる 来る 走る
A-B-B （過去形と過去 分詞が同じ）	bring buy catch feel have hear keep leave make meet pay say spend stand teach tell think understand	brought bought caught felt had heard kept left made met paid said spent stood taught told thought understood	brought bought caught felt had heard kept left made met paid said spent stood taught told thought understood	bringing buying catching feeling having hearing keeping leaving making meeting paying saying spending standing teaching telling thinking understanding	持ってくる 買う 捕まえる 感じる 持っている 聞く 保つ 立ち去る 作る 会う 払う 言う 過ごす 立つ 教える 話す 思う 理解する
A-B-C （原形、過去形、過去分詞が すべて異なる）	be begin break choose drink eat fall get give go know see speak take write	was/were began broke chose drank ate fell got gave went knew saw spoke took wrote	been begun broken chosen drunk eaten fallen gotten/got given gone known seen spoken taken written	being beginning breaking choosing drinking eating falling getting giving going knowing seeing speaking taking writing	〜である 始まる 壊す 選ぶ 飲む 食べる 落ちる 手に入れる 与える 行く 知っている 見る 話す 取る 書く

▟ 音節 ▟

　音節とは、簡単に言うと、「母音を中心とした音のかたまり」で、[ái] といった二重母音も 1 つの母音と考えます。hot [hát] や big [bíg] などのごく短い単語は 1 音節ですが、strike [stráik] など、一見長そうに見える単語でも母音は [ái] しかありませんので、実は 1 音節です。

　単語が何音節であるかは、辞書に載っています。例えば、interesting を辞書で調べてみると、in・ter・est・ing のように区切られて表示されており、この区切りが音節の区切りを示しています。したがって、interesting は 4 音節だとわかります。

　慣れるまでは辞書で確かめるようにしてください。

発音記号の読み方① 母音編

■母音と子音

「母音」とは、日本語の「アイウエオ」のように、肺から出る空気が舌や歯、唇などに邪魔されずに自由に口から出る音のことです。これに対して、「子音」とは、喉から出る息や声が途中でいろいろと邪魔されて、口や鼻から出る音のことです。

■有声音と無声音

声帯が振動する音のことを「有声音」と言い、逆に声帯が振動しない音のことを「無声音」と言います。母音はすべて有声音ですが、子音には有声音と無声音の両方があります。

CD 2-16,17

短母音	[ɑ]	口を思いきり開け口の奥の方から「ア」。	box / hot
	[ʌ]	口をあまり開けない「ア」。	come / bus
	[ə]	口を軽く開けて弱く「ア」。	woman / about
	[æ]	「エ」の口の形で「ア」。	bank / hand
	[i]	日本語の「イ」と「エ」の中間。	sick / it
	[i:]	唇を左右に引いて「イー」。	see / chief
	[u]	[u:]よりも少し唇をゆるめて「ウ」。	good / look
	[u:]	唇を小さく丸めて「ウー」。	school / two
	[e]	日本語の「エ」とほぼ同じ。	net / desk
	[ɔ:]	口を大きく開け唇を少し丸めて「オー」。	talk / ball
	[a:r]	口を大きく開けて「アー」の後、舌先を巻き上げた音を添える。	large / far
	[ə:r]	口を軽く開けて「アー」の後、舌先を巻き上げた音を添える。	girl / work
二重母音	[ei]	始めの音を強く発音し、後の音は軽く添える感じで、「エィ」。	game / say
	[ɔi]	上と同じ感じで、「オィ」。	boy / oil
	[ai]	上と同じ感じで、「アィ」。	write / kind
	[au]	上と同じ感じで、「アゥ」。	house / now
	[ou]	上と同じ感じで、「オゥ」。	boat / cold
	[iər]	「イァ」に舌先を巻き上げた音を添える。	dear / hear
	[eər]	「エァ」に舌先を巻き上げた音を添える。	air / bear
	[uər]	「ウァ」に舌先を巻き上げた音を添える。	poor / tour

発音記号の読み方② 子音編

破裂音	[p]	「パ」行子音とほぼ同じ。	pen / cup
	[b]	[p] の有声音。「バ」行子音とほぼ同じ。	big / job
	[t]	「タ」行子音とほぼ同じ。	tea / meet
	[d]	[t] の有声音。「ダ」行子音とほぼ同じ。	day / food
	[k]	「カ」行子音とほぼ同じ。	cook / take
	[g]	[k] の有声音。「ガ」行子音とほぼ同じ。	game / leg
摩擦音	[f]	下唇を上の歯にあて、息を出して「フ」。	five / enough
	[v]	[f] の有声音で、「ヴ」。	voice / wave
	[θ]	舌先を前歯で軽く噛むようにして「ス」。	think / month
	[ð]	[θ] の有声音で、「ズ」。	there / brother
	[s]	「サ、ス、セ、ソ」の子音とほぼ同じ。	sea / nice
	[z]	[s] の有声音で、「ザ、ズ、ゼ、ゾ」の子音とほぼ同じ。	zoo / lose
	[ʃ]	「シ」とほぼ同じ。	she / fish
	[ʒ]	[ʃ] の有声音で、「ジ」。	usual / vision
	[h]	「ハー」と息を吹きかけてガラスを曇らせるときのような「ハ」。	hot / hand
破擦音	[tʃ]	「チャ」「チュ」「チョ」の子音とほぼ同じ。	church / watch
	[dʒ]	[tʃ] の有声音で、「ヂャ」「ヂュ」「ヂョ」の子音とほぼ同じ。	join / edge
鼻音	[m]	「マ」行子音とほぼ同じ。	meet / time
	[n]	舌の先を上の歯茎につけて、鼻から息を出す。	noon / run
	[ŋ]	[g] を言うつもりで、鼻から声を出す。	thing / song
側音	[l]	必ず舌の先を上の歯茎につける。	late / wall
移行音	[r]	「ウ」のように唇をすぼめる感じで、舌先は歯茎につけない。	red / marry
	[w]	唇をよく丸めて発音する。	way / quick
	[j]	「ヤ、ユ、ヨ」の子音とほぼ同じ。	young / beyond

∥ QR コードの URL 一覧 ∥

Unit 1	Officer's Role Takashi's Role	https://youtu.be/rH5OmvrN1HQ https://youtu.be/eJEJTBtO6nE
Unit 2	Officer's Role Takashi's Role	https://youtu.be/OiZ1OVc-8Ps https://youtu.be/0gl_I8HZ1Oo
Unit 3	Donna's Role Takashi's Role	https://youtu.be/hHrcK5PG7jE https://youtu.be/mDvcJFJkC5Q
Unit 4	Donna's Role Takashi's Role	https://youtu.be/xTDiwoGPVO0 https://youtu.be/I7Ymb2QTwMw
Unit 5	Takashi's Role Beth's Role	https://youtu.be/3KLp2r6IJd8 https://youtu.be/ZE7dwQSwP6s
Unit 6	Donna's Role Takashi's Role	https://youtu.be/IgV24HlhWQM https://youtu.be/Br8jz2L4Dl8
Unit 7	Server's Role Takashi's Role	https://youtu.be/jexITdrCjZE https://youtu.be/9G0SdBqP4-0
Unit 8	Doctor's Role Takashi's Role	https://youtu.be/UkXJxxFO_Yg https://youtu.be/6jQL8e16hHA
Unit 9	Takashi's Role Passerby's Role	https://youtu.be/_f-JBfIzb5c https://youtu.be/i9of0li439Y
Unit 10	Takashi's Role Tourist's Role	https://youtu.be/45RS2v3W8p4 https://youtu.be/JwCNGP4aEx8
Unit 11	Takashi's Role Clerk's Role	https://youtu.be/pVS1DcFueGg https://youtu.be/6TZQ6_PWlxU
Unit 12	Takashi's Role Yoona's Role	https://youtu.be/m9k8bTVBjX8 https://youtu.be/8ijb43uG_40
Unit 13	Takashi's Role Yoona's Role Donna's Role	https://youtu.be/M4jAbijXZLg https://youtu.be/WEKPrI760AU https://youtu.be/Pfu4mNAS_Tc
Unit 14	Clerk's Role Takashi's Role	https://youtu.be/CxI_HXynqIs https://youtu.be/OnGJL5txYDs
Unit 15	Takashi's Role Donna's Role	https://youtu.be/Aph8gVL3CmA https://youtu.be/fKwqbxKFD8w

TEXT PRODUCTION STAFF

edited by   編集
Minako Hagiwara   萩原 美奈子
Takashi Kudo   工藤 隆志

cover design by   表紙デザイン
Nobuyoshi Fujino   藤野 伸芳

illustration by   イラスト
Yoko Sekine   関根 庸子

CD PRODUCTION STAFF

recorded by   吹き込み者
Jack Merluzzi (AmE)   ジャック・マルージ（アメリカ英語）
Rachel Walzer (AmE)   レイチェル・ワルザー（アメリカ英語）
Yuki Minatsuki (JPN)   水月 優希（日本語）

Let's Read Aloud & Learn English: Going Abroad
音読で学ぶ基礎英語《海外生活編》

2021年1月20日　初版発行
2024年3月5日　第5刷発行

著　者　角山 照彦　Simon Capper　遠藤 利昌
発行者　佐野 英一郎
発行所　株式会社 成美堂
〒101-0052　東京都千代田区神田小川町3-22
TEL 03-3291-2261　FAX 03-3293-5490
https://www.seibido.co.jp

印刷・製本　三美印刷(株)

ISBN 978-4-7919-7226-5　　　　　　　Printed in Japan